THE CENTRAL PROBLEM OF ECONOMICS

THE CENTRAL PROBLEM
OF
ECONOMICS
(ECONOMICS REDEFINED)

DR. AMITAVA MUKHERJEE
Adviser
District Planning Unit
Lal Bahadur Shastri National Academy of Administration,
(Government of India)
Mussoorie

CONCEPT PUBLISHING COMPANY, NEW DELHI-110059

ISBN 81-7022-347-4

First Published 1991

Published and Printed by
Ashok Kumar Mittal
Concept Publishing Company
A/15-16, Commercial Block, Mohan Garden
NEW DELHI-110059 (India)

Lasertypeset by
Microtech Advance Printing Systems (Pvt.) Ltd.
H-13, Bali Nagar
NEW DELHI-110015

To
My Mother
Who Taught Me

"The happiness of the whole is the result of
the happiness of individuals,
and to begin first with them . . . Eery step tells.
He who performs his duty faithfully
will reap the full fruit of it,
whatever may be the number of others who fail."

CONTENTS

"FOR WHOM THE BELL TOLLS"

What Economics is all about has agitated great minds. For a long time the *title* of Adam Smith's monumented work *An Enquiry into the Nature and Causes of Wealth of Nations*[1] was taken as articulating the principal focus of Economics. Though Economics was continuously evolving ever since Smith published his work and economic theory underwent radical transformation then on, the definition of economics and the principal tasks of the Economists remained unchanged for nearly a century and a half, notwithstanding the exceptionally brilliant attempt of the "Young Curate" living in the lovely valley between North Downs and Leith Hill, named Thomas Robert Malthus, to steer the focus of economics in another direction, in his epoch making work, *An Essay on the Principles of Population or a View of its Past and Present Effect on Human Happiness with an Inquiry into our Prospects Respecting the Future Removal or Mitigation of the Evils which it Occasions*,[2] which has been termed by the great Alfred Marshall as "one of the most crushing answers that patient and hardworking Science has ever given to the reckless assertions of its adversaries".[3]

The first breach in the ancient wall appeared with the emergence of Lionel Robbin's polemical masterpiece *An Essay on the Nature and Significance of Economic Science*,[4] in the second year of "the decade noted for great controversies in economics",[5] namely 1932, where he led a frontal attack on the conception of economics as an enquiry into the nature and causes of wealth of nations. And following his pronouncements, economists accepted that Economics was "a science which studies human behaviour as a relationship between (a given hierarchy of) ends and scarce means which have alternative uses".[6] Thus the fundamental problem of economics was conceived of as the matching the hierarchy of ends to limited resources, which have alternative uses. That is, Economists were concerned with the crucial problem of scarcity. Lionel Robbins himself forty years after writing his *Essay*, published his *Autobiography*[7] which gave him a rare opportunity of having at least a fleeting glimpse of the reception his ideas had received but it seems he remained unpersuaded by the criticism labelled against his thoughts. A long chain of economists, including Samuelson, himself thereafter attempted a modification of the definition of economics:

> "On first encountering economics, people often want a short definition. In response to this demand, there is no shortage of supply. Here are a few popular definitions:
>
> Economics is the study of those activities that involve production and exchange among people.
>
> Economics analyzes movements in the overall economy-trends in prices, output, and unemployment. Once such phenomena are understood, economics helps develop the policies by which governments can affect the overall economy.
>
> Economics is the science of choice. It studies

how people choose to use *Scarce or limited* productive resources (land, labour, equipment, technical knowledge) to produce various commodities (such as wheat, beef, overcoats, concerts, roads, missiles) and distribute these goods to various members of society for their consumption.

Economics is the study of how human beings go about the business of organizing consumption and production activities.

Economics is the study of money interest rates, capital, and wealth.

The list is a good one, yet a scholar can extend it many times over. Why is it so long ? Because, for a subject that encompasses so much and evolves so rapidly, it is always hard to compress into a few lines an exact description that will differentiate its boundaries from those of other disciplines. Economics certainly does involve all the elements stressed in these various definitions - and more".[8]

But they eventually went on to write that:

> "Economics is the study of how people and society choose to employ scarce resources that could have alternative uses in order to produce various commodities and to distribute them for consumption, now or in the future, among various persons and groups in society."[9]

Clearly enough the basic problem of Economics in terms of its redefinition by Samuelson and *et al.*, continues to be largely in the domain of choosing the employment of *scarce resources* that could have *alternative uses* for producing goods and services. The dominant strand remains the scarcity element "invented" by Lionel Robbins.

In a world where the paradox of plenty and poverty persists and where surplus men, material and technology is rampant, it is futile to circumscribe the concern of economists to tackling the scarcity problem alone. Unless economists can redefine their position and redelineate their principal focus on solving the "paradox" presented by the co-existence of poverty and plenty, their science will drift further away from the realities which confront homo sapiens. This work is directed towards attempting such a redefinition though tentative.

There shall be four chapters in the book. *Chapter 1* will present the problematic. *Chapter 2* will define the surplus problem. *Chapter 3* will deal with the sources of the surplus problem. *Chapter 4* will be a tentative outline of the course of action to tackle, albeit partially, the surplus problem.

In the preparation of this work I have largely depended upon the resources available at Charleville. The assistance received from of Fondren Library, Rice University, Houston, Texas, is gratefully acknowledged. Dr. G.K. Iyer, Professor of Sociology, Punjab University, Chandigarh deserves my thanks for his helpful comments. My friend, Dr. N.R. Farooqui Professor, LBS National Academy of Administration, Mussoorie read some parts of the manuscript and offered helpful suggestions. He is thanked. Dr. (Mrs.) Neela Mukherjee, Professor of Economics, National Academy of Administration, Charleville, Mussoorie has been always supportive of my activities. My thanks to her. Finally thanks are due to Shri M.K. Tyagi for his fine assistance.

The usual dislaimer applies: I am alone responsible for all the errors that remain.

Lal Bahadur Shastri AMITAVA MUKHERJEE
National Academy of Administration,
Charleville, MUSSOORIE
23rd October 1990.

NOTES

1. Adam Smith: *An Enquiry into the Nature & Causes of Wealth of Nations* (London: Straham & Cadell) 1976.
2. Thomas Robert Malthus: *An Essay on the Principle of Population or a View of its Past and Present Effect on Human Happiness with an Inquiry into our Prospects Respecting the Future Removal or Mitigation of the Evils which it occasions*, (London: John Murray) Vol.I & II (Sixth Edition) 1826.
3. Alfred Marshall: *The Economics of Industry* (London : MacMillan & Co.) Second Edition, 1805, p. 30.
4. Lionel Robbins: *An Essay on the Nature and Significance of Economic Science* (London : MacMillan) 1932, Second Edition 1935.
5. Mark Blaugh: *The Methodology of Economics or How Economists Explain* (Cambridge : Cambridge University Press) 1980, reprinted 1985, p. 90.
6. Lionel Robbins: *loc. cit*, pp. 16 - 17.
7. Lionel Robbins: *Autobiography of an Economist* (London : MacMillan)1971.
8. Paul A. Samuelson and William D. Nordhaus: *Economics* (Singapore: McGraw Hill Book Co.), International Student 1985.
9. *Idem.*

1

THE PROBLEMATIC

Introduction

This short book will attempt at bringing forth the need for a redirection of the interests of economists from the study of the allocation of scarce resources among competing ends within the limits set by various conceptions of equilibrium analysis to the study of the integration and coordination of men, technology, and materials into a problem-solving verifiable continuum, and attempt at a redefinition of economics as a study of how to solve the problem of surplus, men, material and technology, as opposed to a study of how to solve the problem of matching scarce resources with unlimited wants.

In this chapter 1 we shall examine where the economists failed; in chapter 2 we would examine the problem of surplus and in chapter 3 we shall attempt at investigating the sources of surplus and the reasons why economics should be redefined as a study of tackling the surplus problem as stated above Chapter 4 will have a policy proposal.

Where Economists Failed

There exists a curious paradox of having, coincidentally, a surplus and a scarcity of the same goods in the world, and considerable confusion arises out of the necessity of concurrently tackling the problem of surplus, say of food, and the problem of a scarcity, say of food again. The capitalistic system to survive and sustain the democratic super-structure, which provides the justification for being called the most fruitful economic organization of society yet devised, must find a solution to the paradox of scarcity amidst surplus.

The co-existence of market surpluses of goods and services, with at once, large mass of humanity suffering for lack of them,[1] has been caused by failure to clearly understand how the economy works. Obviously, when reference is made to the same set of commodities by both expressions, a surplus can coexist with scarcity only by defining the two terms upon different basis and opposing value systems.

The fact, therefore, that man has so organized his efforts to manage his economic affairs that surplus and scarcity, perpetually and concurrently occur, clearly indicates the bifurcation in human behaviour and culture. A part of the behaviour is grounded in verifiable beliefs and serves to produce verifiable results which admit of objective evaluation in terms of the past, the present, and the anticipated existential situation and a part of behaviour is built upon myth and often serves to prevent intelligent and verifiable behaviour.

Instead of producing and distributing goods by a

continuous process of verifiable decisions, man has not succeeded in using all the means available to him to solve the problems which have afflicted him. For the most part, economists have offered purportedly logical explanations of this failure of man to solve the problems that have troubled him, and they have not only condoned this failure but have additionally attempted to perpetuate the belief that it is both a natural and an almost inevitable state of affairs. Thus, economics, in large part, could not succeed in fulfilling the rigid requirements of science, and one reason for this failure has been that economists have persistently and unquestioningly accepted some of the unverifiable beliefs of their predecessors in calling. The principal preconceptions that need to be re-evaluated is the faith that the productive process of the human species would receive its most effective direction from a natural or automatic distributive process.

Economists, by assuming that some given behaviour pattern of man is "natural" and that such behaviour pattern provides optimum organization of human activity, arrived at the conclusion that their discipline can be a positive science, but not a normative one. If the problem of organizing human activity is assumed to rest with some power other than man (or his culture) only then it can be concluded that science is not the source of intelligent value judgments. Because the science began with the assumption that an equilibrium generated by the system of markets and prices provides optimum utilization of men, technology, and materials, recognition and definition of economic problems have been made largely in terms of deviations from the ideal to an automatic distributive process, but reliance upon the assumption that the equilibrium generated by the system of markets and prices would ensure the most effective utilization of man's economic activities has led, on the one hand, Economists to define economics as the study of the allocation of scarce resources among competing ends; and, on the other society has been ceaselessly engaged in adjusting the productive system to a distributive system that leaves unabsorbed some goods which could be produced by the most efficient techniques available.

No society has ever succeeded in approaching full utilization of all the labour, technology and materials available to it, because of the ineffective organization of human efforts. Acceptance of the efficacy of values received out of the past which are not verifiable, has been the cornerstone on which human activity has been organised which, inhibits the intelligent organization of human behaviour. The distributive process that has been relied upon by the economists, invariably has not been capable of organizing human efforts, and of distributing the products of all the available productive elements. The productive process, in turn has been adjusted to the partially ineffective distributive system.

Economist's Real Problem

The economist's real problem is to discover how the available resources: men, technology, and materials, which are not now being effectively organized, admit of integration and co-ordination into the economic activity of homo sapiens. In short, economic theory should be directed towards solving the surplus problem, the unused resources, both material and labour, and know-how, that are available for use in alleviating the problems that emerge in the process of man's attempts at making a living.

The principal problems of the capitalistic economies is the development of a distributive system which is adjustable to the productive process, and stop adjusting the productive process to the distributive system. The fact that the capitalistic system has become intimately associated with a distributive process based upon income distribution, explains why the problem necessarily boils down to a necessity of modifying the income-price distributive system in order that it will no longer necessarily embody the surplus problem. Till such time as this problem is clearly identified and tackled, and with concerted effort in the near future, the capitalistic societies are likely to become a stagnant eddy in the backwash of cultural progress.

The ideas that will occur implicitly or explicitly in the paper would be hopefully a part of the cultural heritage of our generation. It is to be hoped that it will be possible to combine them in a manner that will encourage more verifiable behaviour and not perpetuate that part of the past which is nonsense.

NOTE

1. "Though there is sufficient food for everyone, 500 million people are still suffering from hunger and disease and even die because they are too poor to buy the food that is already there. . . . The obese are seeking new cures and

the malnourished are offered no remedies. Many pets are pampered while hungry children are forgotten. Is this not a strange phenomenon that historians and economists of future times will undoubtedly consider mysterious and inexplicable?" Edouard Saouma, Director General, Food and Agriculture Organisation of the United Nations, on the occasion of the 2nd World Food Day, Rome, October 16th, 1982.

2

THE PROBLEM OF SURPLUSES

System of Markets and Prices

Economics unfortunately has been conceived as dealing with problems of scarcity. "Economics is a science which studies human behaviour as a relationship between . . . ends and scarce means which have alternative uses."[1] This is because of the peculiar assumptions upon which it has been built since the eighteenth-century Age of Reason. Economics has been so defined as the study of the man in his attempt at securing his livelihood, but economics has scarcely approached such a study due to the restrictions imposed by the starting assumptions: (i) that man's efforts to make a living are organized by a system of markets and prices; (ii) that they can be organized in no other way; (iii) that the purpose and tendency of the system markets and prices is to maintain equilibrium, and (iv) that equilibrium prices produce the most effective organization of man's activities to satisfy his wants and needs.

The assumption that equilibrium prices automatically provide the most efficient possible organization of the economic leads us to the conclusion that economics is logically confined to the study of prices, and things not measurable by the system of markets and prices, in terms of prices are, therefore, not-economic and of no consequence to the organization of human activities directed towards making a living. Economists for long has sought to describe the pattern formed by a price system in equilibrium, but subsequently price economists went even beyond to attempt at a description of the actual workings of the system of markets and prices, and to show how it deviates from the model that was essential to effectively maintain the equilibrium.

The purposes of the system of markets and prices are indeed to maintain equilibrium, and the creation of an equilibrium model. The study of the variations of actual prices from the ideal equilibrium conditions is a legitimate area for investigation by economists, but too many errors have crept in while interpreting the importance of the price system and its study. The study of prices and the price system is the study not of how man seeks his livelihood, but the study of how prices are determined in the market at particularly point in time, in the evolution of this particular society. It is an amazingly restricted study of only one segment of the wide gamut of human behaviour. It is patently wrong to assume that equilibrium prices are utopia.

The assumptions that the price system seeks equilibrium, that equilibrium prices provide perfect coordination of human efforts to maintain the continuation of whatever man values most, and that no other forces are involved in the performance of this function, has led to the conclusion that the deviations of the actual operations of the price system from the equilibrium model is a problem which needs to be solved by a "return" to equilibrium. Economic theory has, therefore, been not only largely inaccurate and misleading, but it has been at times been even detrimental to the welfare of man. In itself, much of economic theory has been turned into a series of esoteric exercises in rigour, undertaken for the aesthetic amusement of those who feel they have nothing better to do. While there is nothing innately wrong in deriving such pleasures, but when an important area such as the study of how man goes about the process of living is appropriated as the pasture for pleasantries, and other disciplines which could produce meaningful conclusions are excluded, the situation is fraught with danger. The continuation of the human species, that is, the life-process of man, may be allowed to deteriorate with no one very much more wiser and with no forewarning of the developments underway.

Once economic theory starts questioning the validity of the basic premise that equilibrium prices produce the most efficient organisation of human efforts to secure its livelihood, economics will be seen to be wider in scope than the system of markets and prices and the avenues for investigation will be clear, which will produce analyses of how man's attempts at making a livelihood are actually organized, how successful these attempts have been, and how such future attempts could be improved upon. Economics will be freed of the inflexibility that have circumvented every consideration of all the factors involved in the totality of human behaviour. Dropping the assumption that equilibrium prices are the source of all good things, will lead to considerations of what equilibrium prices actually are, what results such equilibrium prices produce, and how these equilibrium prices are related to the important function of making a living.

The End-Means Continuum

Rational human behaviour is organized activity aimed at producing desired, verifiable results, which in turn, will serve as the means of arriving at further desired, verifiable ends. This continuous process of coordinating activity producing a new state of affairs that precludes problematic situations embodied in earlier stages of the developing organization of activities, constitutes the ends-means continuum, which is called the "process of instrumental valuation," which involves the following steps:-

(i) A recognition of an empirical problematic situation.
(ii) An empirical analysis of the conditions presently obtaining which produces an awareness of a problematic situation and a definition of conditions that would eliminate the undesired situation.
(iii) An appraisal of the desired conditions, namely, the end-in-view, so as to anticipate the consequences of that organization of activities.
(iv) An analysis of the alternative means available which is essential for choosing those means which will actually achieve the desired end, if the expected consequences of the end-in-view are found to be acceptable.
(v) An appraisal of the means necessary to determine how far the means are acceptable as intermediate ends-in-view.
(vi) A continual comparison between the achieved and warranted results must be made as the

chosen hypothesis is acted upon, because the resulting contrast gives a clearer view about the fitness of the means and the acceptability of the end. The adequacy or otherwise, of each end-in-view is a function of the correspondence between the warranted and achieved results and the effectiveness with which the problematic situation is eliminated. It is at this point in the process of instrumental valuation that the identity of means and ends is most clearly revealed. Every end serves as a means of attaining further ends, and every means is employed as an end from which to proceed by other means to further ends.

(vii) Theories are generated, from the working out of such attempts at eliminating problematic situations, which profess to present a scenario of the relationship of means to their actual consequences, and general observations are presented about the acceptability of means employed and values prized by the society as ends.

If economics is to be of an value, it has to be a tool of analysis, to assist in directing attempts at selecting as ends-in-view only desires which are empirically verifiable and which, when viewed from the standpoint of expected consequences, opens the possibility of becoming means to further desired ends. Economics can be usefully employed in appraising the warranted situations to be brought about and the means of attaining these ends-in-view, only to the extent, that it ensures more accurate estimates of the relationship of means to their actual consequences.

Thus economic theory must succeed in providing a thread bare analysis of the actual conditions that embody a problematic situation, delineate the new coordination of activities essential for circumventing the problematic situation, and provide the means to reach this end-in-view. Economic theory can hope to achieve this, provided traditions, customs, usage, emotional loyalties, superstitions, prejudices, received values, and other aspects of the situation obtaining, are all subjected to empirical investigation: acceptance of any part of the scenario as given and beyond question, may lead to the acceptance of the very conditions that are germane to the problematic situation. The point of departure for such an analysis must be an understanding of the existing cultural elements which has been handed down to society by foregoing generations and received from past societies. It is only then that it will be possible to examine the inter-relationships determined behaviour patterns and problematic situations.

Culture and Human Behaviour

All meaningful theory attempting at dealing with human behaviour from any perspective must have a study of the culture, or the socially transmitted sum of man-made physical objects, beliefs, and understanding, which has generated the behaviour, as the starting point. The nature of any pattern of human behaviour can be understood only through an understanding of the cultural elements that have gone into the production of such behaviour. Society always has some explanation for any pattern of human behaviour, but, more often than not such explanations are myths. Neither the cause, nor the purpose, nor the actual results of any behaviour pattern can be accurately determined, in whatever manner, other than through the study of the cultural context in which it was born, and through the study of the other cultural elements, which in its turn is affected by the behaviour, and by which it is itself again affected. The need for beginning an examination of human bahaviour with the analysis of culture, emanates so powerfully because:

> Human organisms live in a cultural environment. There is no desire and no interest which, in its distinction from raw impulse and strictly organic appetite, is not what it is because of transformation effeted in the latter by their interaction with the cultural environment. When current theories are examined which, quite properly, relate valuation with desires and interest, nothing is more striking than their neglect (so extensive as to be systematic) of the role of cultural conditions and institutions in the shaping of desires and ends and thereby of valuations. . . . Furthermore, the notion that an adequate theory of human behaviour including particularly the phenomena of desire and purpose can be formed by considering individuals apart from the cultural setting in which they live, move, and have their being, a theory which can justly be called metaphysical individualism--has united with the metaphysical belief in a mentalistic realm to keep valuation-phenomena in subjection to unexamined traditions, conventions, and institutionalised customs.[2]

Because economic theory of markets and prices

is based upon the acceptance of the existing culture as an immutable and impenetrable enclosure, to the nearly total exclusion of the analysis of culture. Economics produces analyses of empirical situations in terms of the values and traditions embodied in existing institutions. Knowledge of a problematic situation produces its definition, in terms of a departure from an *a priori* ideal, which is assumed to be an organisation of activities bereft of any problematic situations, while in reality, it is indeed an organisation of activities which perpetuates the existing culture configuration, including the source of the problems under reference.

Because economics arrives at the conclusion that the real trouble is the deviation from an ultimate ideal and because it sees this ideal as an end in itself, it precludes all possibilities of determining the true nature of the problematic situation, of defining a revised organisation of activities in terms of the existential situation that could serve as a verifiable solution, and of awareness and appraisal of all the means available. Economic price theory accepts an ultimate ideal as an end, and it, therefore, additionally prevents the necessary continual appraisal of the past consequences of acting on its hypotheses.

The absence of verifiability in economic price theory, which wipes out any utility it might have as a tool of analysis in the problem solving continuum, results from a failure to recognize the relationship between existing values, traditions, and institutions (reflected in actual behaviour) to empirical organisations of activity embodying problematic situations. No theory of human behaviour that accepts the existing culture, with its embodied values, beliefs, and institutions, as constant, can have the attribute of verifiability, because culture is dynamic, it continually changes, and because human being is a product of his culture. A pre-requisite for acceptable theories of human behaviour, which can satisfy inviolable criterion of verifiability, is an understanding of the actual cause and the effect of particular patterns of human behaviour. A clear understanding of why a certain behaviour pattern occurs is possible only through a study of the relationship of the cultural elements that produce it, to other cultural elements, a study which invariably involves the history of the cultural elements.

Men, Material and Tool Process

All that is necessary for man to produce, whatever he wants, is the materials from which to create the project, the tools which with to shape the materials, and the knowledge (technology) necessary to organize the men, tools, and materials into a successful productive effort. Because the ability of man to produce what he wants is a function of the use of men, technology, and materials, economic theory ought to be concerned with their availability and use. Unemployed men, surplus goods, and idle capacity, all remind us that all of the factors of production available to man may not be put to good use, i.e., they may not be integrated into the functioning economy. The existence of farms too small to be operated efficiently, the production of goods and services detrimental to human welfare, and the use of obsolete equipment are constant reminders to us that not only must the available men, materials and technology be used but they must also be appropriately coordinated with other parts of the economy into a harmonious whole to be most effective.

Economic theory, following Lionel Robbins, assumes a scarcity of means, but observation of the actual conditions that are obtaining today, indicates that while there are some men, technology, and materials that are not used at all, there are others that are used ineffectively, ineffeciently and incapably. Therefore, economics can be re-defined not as a study of allocating limited means to unlimited wants, but as the study of the effectiveness with which men, their tools and know-how, and the available materials are integrated and coordinated into a problem solving means-end continuum, namely, a tool-process. When the totality of human behaviour is viewed from this perspective, the real problem of economics is seen to be one of surplus, and not of scarcity. When economics is taken as the study of the technical operation of the tool-process, "surplus" denotes the existence of men, technology or materials, which have not been integrated into the tool-process, or where partially integrated, have been left un-coordinated such that they do not form an effectively functioning part of the problem-solving means-end continuum.

The instrumental organism produced by the organization of men, technology, and materials into a functioning network of interrelated parts is termed the "tool process," and the continuous organization of the elements of the "tool-process" is a problem of dynamic development. The available quantities of men, material and technology change, the nature of the various elements change, and the degrees of interdependence of the myriad parts of the aggregate tool-process is in a state of constant flux. The effectiveness with which the network of inter-related parts is organized into a functioning whole is also subject to change. The tool-process, is therefore an evolving technological complex characterized by an ever-improving organization of activities, i.e., a more effective integration and coordination of its elements, and the very fact that the life-process of man is supported by the tool-process, enjoins that the tool-process be the subject matter of economics.

While the tool-process is a continuum 'an evolving organization of activities' its internal organization is observable at any point in its evolution, which is necessary for determining the effectiveness with which the elements of the process are currently being organized and how its integration and coordination could possibly be improved, if the price integration and co-ordination is incomplete. Economic theory of markets and prices, correctly attempt at describing the organization of the tool-process, 'at least partially', at a particular point in its evolution, but where it erred was that it started of with the invalid presumption of a static model, rather than from the understanding of the evolving tool process, which error has resulted in the distorted conception of society as being bound only by "scarcity of means", rather than viewing society as being limited by internal maladjustments that prevents the integration and effective coordination of all men, material and technology available into the functioning economy.

If attention is focused on the need for improving the organization of the tool-process, that is, of co-ordinating men, material and technology, the problem of economics really turns out to be one of managing surplus. The scarcity of means assumption of price economics, not only misleads but it also precludes all hopes of alleviating problem areas without impairing the welfare of other areas. The problem of economics is concerned with the most effective use possible of the available components of the tool-process, and while attempting to achieve the most effective use of the available components of the tool process, the dynamic nature of the tool-process will itself generate a continual expansion of the manpower, technology, and materials available for being integrated and coordinated.

The population now existing is sufficient for the tool-process, and the manpower available from this population will increase continuously as machines are developed to perform more of the tasks previously executed by men and as studies in medicine extends the life expectancy of man. Whether the birth rate should be such as to maintain, reduce or increase, the existing population is a function of the capacity of society to integrate and effectively coordinate the available manpower into the tool process. This capacity will vary with different societies and with the same society at different times.

In societies characterized by primitive or less advanced technology and characterised by an extremely high birth rate, attempts at encouraging birth control for reducing the magnitude of the problem that will arise when sanitation and medical knowledge suddenly lower the mortality rate, would be the appropriate course of action. Contrarily, past experience has taught us that the same technical progress that brought about rapid population growth, by suddenly lowering the death rate, also reduces the birth rate as the society moves from an outfit of less advanced technology towards a more industrialised structure.[3] A rapidly expanding population, therefore, is likely to be only a transitional problem, though the span of the transitory period could be different for different countries.

Surplus, Technology and Welfare

The level of technology currently used determines the welfare of any society. Technology is inherently dynamic since the tools and concepts come together in unique combinations as men absorb culture. At times these combinations of tools and concepts occur per chance, that is, accidental discovery, while at other times they may be caused by scientific experimentation or from the native activity of individuals with hardly any training in the characteristics, limits and procedures for using the tools and concepts they are instrumental in combining. The native activity of individuals, accounts for a good deal of the rapid progress that often occurs when the technical heritage of one culture configuration is diffused to an area of lower cultural elements where preconceptions about the technology of the more advanced culture is non-existing and is dominated by non-verifiable beliefs which have grown up around the pivot of technology and serve to perpetuate the past. No society could have more technology than would be beneficial for it, if the technology were integrated and effectively coordinated, and therefore, irrespective of how much the existing organization of activities falls short of that state of affairs, the strength and magnitude of the inhibiting beliefs for allowing as much non-verifiable behaviour as was possible, should be reduced, or at least attempts made in that direction.

The materials available to be integrated and coordinated into the tool-process, which includes the goods that are produced by the Society *plus* what is called natural resources, will continually increase because they are a product of technology.

Production of goods and services can be carried out up to the "point" where the amount of goods available equals the amount of goods desired, for the effective coordination of the tool-process, but beyond that level of production, more leisure is preferable to more goods.

The resources available are created by advancing technology. Some resources, such as the solar energy, have been termed "renewable" or "flow resources" because they are continuously renewed as they are used, and failure to use what is available today is to lose it forever, which is why there is no question of conserving renewable or flow resources. Resources not constantly renewed, such as coal gas and petroleum, have been termed as "non-renewable" or "fund resources",[4] but man has seldom been faced in history with the problem of exhausting the available supplies of "non-renewable" or "fund resources" because, *one*, advancement in technology often discovers and ensures the recovery of additional quantities of non-renewable resources at a faster rate than they are consumes, and, *two*, before a non-renewable or fund resource becomes scarce, technology advances to a stage where non-renewable or fund resource is no longer used in great amounts or alternative non-renewable resources have been developed as substitutes. This has occurred in the past with such things as flint and is occurring today as light metals replace some of the heavy metals or as solar energy replaces coal or petroleum energy. Taken as a whole and viewed historically the distinction between non-renewable or fund resources and renewable or flow resources is clearly blurred.

It is true that man has never been confronted with the problem of resource being completely exhausted, but that in no way offers unbridled sanctions that resources should be wasted recklessly with a prodigal hand : resources should be used according to the need to achieve an ever-improving organization of the tool-process because over-use of a resource may partake the nature of non-optimal use of men and technology even though the resource may not be limited in the strict sense of the term.

Economist's fear of the lack of additional amounts of the elements of the tool-process, namely, of men, technology and materials, can be justified only where no possibility exists of further integration of these elements into the tool process, or improvements in the coordination of the existing tool-process. Because that state of development may not be reached, the real problem of economics is that of effectively using the already available stock of men, technology and materials.

Throughout recorded history men, technology, and materials have been available that were not properly coordinated into the tool-process. Without exception, in every society that have developed specialized technology to the point of organized towns, a part of the population has been permanently excluded from participation in the functioning economy and these non-integrated men have appeared in society as beggers or vagrants skirting the periphery of society. Additionally there have been idle tools, or if all the tools in existence were in use, the means of producing more in a very short time have been available. Some technology has been withheld from use altogether: it has been the exclusive prerogative of special individuals and denied to the multitudes. And then there is no denying that along with the surplus men and tools, there has always been a surplus stock of goods stacked and stored in warehouses.

The unique feature of a social order which have brought about the exclusion of some of the available elements of the tool-process (men, material and technology) have often prevented the reabsorption of labour whose functions have been usurped by new technology. Technological advancement that have gone in to rapidly increase the productive capacity of society, or have performed tasks previously executed by labour, have often been accompanied by increased surplus, which has been called "technological unemployment." "Technological unemployment" is a misnomer because it carries the implication with it that the increased surplus was caused by technological progress, which was not the case, because the advancing technology led to a more effective coordination of men, material and technology into the tool- process, and it was only an inflexible pattern of institutions and non-verifiable beliefs that prevented the new factors from being integrated into the tool process. The mechanical husker does not cause the people who formerly reaped wheat to be excluded from more fruitful employment, just as the Automated Teller Machine did not cause unemployment of the bank clerks.

Sudden increases in the magnitude of surplus may also accompany a change from one organization of activities to another, as for example, from a self-sufficient agriculture, to a more efficient pattern, namely specialized agriculture. The transition from small and self-sufficient farms to more effective use of tools and land has been so intimately associated and inextricably with production for the market in the past that it has received the appellation of the commercialisation of agriculture. The labourers in the agricultural sector no longer needed for the production of agricultural commodities were made available for an expansion of non-agricultural production. Unfortunately, society has too often allowed production of elaborate commodities which serve no other function than to evidence the importance of the owner, that is for the purposes of what economists have called conspicuous consumption.

Surplus and Economists Concern

Problematic situations arise where evidently additional amounts of some commodity, such as food, are needed. In such circumstance it has to be determined whether less of the commodity is at hand than is required in absolute terms; or less is at hand than could be produced by a more effective organisation of the tool-process: a problem of scarcity would be deemed to exists. However, if more food could be utilised and at once, more could also be made available, by a more effective organisation of the tool process, the problem would get reduced to one of surplus and not of scarcity. The fact of more food being required can be conceived either as a problem of scarcity of food *per se*, or as a problem of surplus men, technology and materials, available for the production of the required quantum of food. While the first approach to the problem will lead to an indeterminate solution, the latter analysis makes the answer to the problem apparent and programmes designed to increase the food availability can be immediately undertaken. In fine, the growing awareness of a need for more of a good merely makes it evident that a surplus problem exists--a surplus of either men, or of technology, or of materials or some combinations of the three. Until awareness of the need for more good arises, the existence of possibilities of providing more has no social significance, and therefore, apparently enough, economics can become more effective in analyzing and improving the way man goes about making a living if the problem with which economics is concerned is approached as a problem of surplus and not of scarcity.

The term "surplus" has received a wide variety of connotations: some use it to refer to commodities produced but which have no buyers, to others the term connotes the production of goods by individuals or combination of individuals, in excess of their "subsistence needs," a term that is difficult to define except broadly in terms of cultural values. Subsistence needs, therefore, are usually accepted as that amount of the factors of a society that are integrated and coordinated into the tool-process, which clearly admits of the possibility that the basic necessities of one society may be greater than or equal to the total of the surplus and necessities of another society.

Every use of the term "surplus" seemingly recognises that a portion of the elements of the tool-process are not integrated and effectively coordinated. A common theme which binds all definitions of the term "surplus" seems to have been a realization that the quantities so designated as being surplus, are distributed and utilized in a manner which is inconsistent with technical considerations of the integration and proper coordination of the tool-process.

It is true that the distinction made here between problems of surplus and the traditionally defined problems of scarcity in economics may be deemed as being merely one of emphasis, but it is just as much true that such a change in the point of emphasis is the necessary condition to generate analyses and instrumental hypotheses which, when acted upon, may alleviate the problems that have become apparent.

The traditional definition of scarcity in economics assumes that human wants are unlimited, that every society is faced with concurrent problems of scarce means pitched against unlimited wants, and that decisions must therefore be made as to which wants will be satisfied first. The assumptions would be open to challenge once the tool process was organized in terms of the verifiable means-end continuum, yet, the more crucial point is that the existing culture embodies non-verifiable values which so inhibit the tool-process that the productive limit of the elements of the tool-process available is never reached, and therefore, more goods could be produced by the integration and effective coordination of the means currently available.

The function of the Economists should be to find ways and means to ameliorate problems by the utilisation of the surplus men, technology, and materials for a more effective organization of the tool-process. The failure of economists to devise ways and means to use all of the elements of the tool-process generates at least three types of non-integration, namely, permanent exclusion, increased exclusion arising as the organization of certain parts of the tool-process is improved, and periodic collapse of the market. The failure to use all the men, technology and materials (elements of the tool-process) gives rise to an exactly equal number of types of ineffective coordination, namely, *one*, deliberate sabotage of the tool-process resulting from some attempts to increase profits and status power,[5] *two*, certain business principles which seek to increase the sales of individual firms in a competitive market, and *three*, substitution of status considerations for technical valuations through ignorance, deliberation, or confusion of non-verifiable with verifiable value judgments.

Wherever the fundamental problem of economists is conceived of as the effective co-ordination of men, technology, and materials into the tool-process, and the existence of problematic situations in which a lack of "something" apparent is recognised as evidence of the existence of surplus elements of the tool-process, economists will succeed in projecting verifiable hypotheses for reducing problematic situations. Until the problem of economics is conceived as problem of surplus rather than scarce means being allocated to unlimited wants, economic theory cannot be either verifiable or useful in solving most problems that baffles the homo sapiens today.

Wants are culturally developed, they do not occur, and they cannot even be conceived of, therefore, until the means of their satisfaction are available, or potentially available, in the foreseeable future, like the cure for a definable disease like cancer. This change in the point of view of economists has more in its favour than against it, because a re-direction of economic thought will result in allowing the definition of a continuum of problems that can be made approachable with the verifiable, experimental methodology of a science. For, . . .

> If the history of science teaches us anything it is that only to those who ask the right questions are any answers vouchsaped. Not even to them are those answers the end of the quest, but only an enlargement and a refining of the question.[6]

Considerable work that is necessary to develop a general theory of surplus in economics has been done, in that the problem of market failures in modern capitalistic nations, particularly so the problem of surplus technology, have been examined, at least in some of their aspects, and a good deal of information has been generated by studies of the surplus problem in agriculture, yet a whole lot remains to be done toward developing a *general theory* for the overall problem, which would lead to a much better understanding of each of the aspects of the general problem.

Because the tool-process, and the surplus problem, are admittedly supra-national in dimension, the problem of the effective integration and coordination of men, technology, and materials into the tool-process must be approached at the international plane, for it will only then become apparent that whatever helps one nation, helps all other nations: one society does not, in the last analysis, better its lot by impairing the welfare of others. There is, loosely speaking, non-existence of the conditions akin to Pareto Optimality in the welfare of the committee of nations.

NOTES

1. Lionnel Robinns : *An Enquiry in to the Nature and Significance of Economic Science* (London: Macmillan) 1930 and his *Autobiography of an Economist* (London : Macmillan) 1971, pp. 16-17. Samuelson and Nordhans has marginally modified Robins definition to state that "Economics is the study of how people and society choose to employ *Scarce resources* that could have *alternative uses* in order to produce various commodities and to distribute them for consumption now or in the future among various persons and groups in society" (Emphasis ours). See Paul A. Samuelson and William D. Nordhans : *Economics*, (Singapore: McGraw Hill Book Co.), International Student Edition, 1985.
2. John Dewey, "Theory of Valuation," *International Encyclopedia of Unified Science*, Vol. II, No. 4, (Chicago : The University of Chicago Press) 1939, pp. 63-64.
3. See Frank W. Notestein, "Population--The Long View", *Food For the World*, edited by Theodore W. Schultz (Chicago : The University of Chicago Press) 1945, which is one of the earlier views on the issue. Subsequently considerable research has gone into it. See Nancy Bidsall: "Analytical Approaches to the Relationship of Population Growth and Development", *Population and Development Review*, Vol. 3, Nos. 1 & 2, March - June 1977, and see also Michael P. Todaro: *Economic Development in the Third World* (London: Longman Group Ltd.) 1981, fourth impression 1984, Chapter 6, Particularly pages 165 to 168.
4. See Erich W. Zimmermann, *World Resources and Industries* (New York : Harpen & Brothers) 1951. And also J.R.C.: "Growth, Resources and Taxation", In Institute of Fiscal Studies: *Proceeding of a Conference on Fiscal Policy and the Environment* (London : Institute of Fiscal Studies) 1974 and Richard Lecomber: *Economic Growth Vs. the Environment* (London : MacMillan) 1978, p. 37.
5. See Thorstein Veblen, *The Engineers and the Price System* (New York : The Viking Press) 1921.
6. William P.D. Wrightman, *The Growth of Scientific Ideas*, (New York : Alfred A. Knopf) 1952, pp. 473-474.

3

THE SOURCE OF SURPLUSES

Verifiable and Mystical Human Behaviour

Errors in the technical organization of men, technology, and materials into a functioning fabric of interrelated parts generates the problem of surpluses, and though technical mistakes in judgment may lead to errors in the technical organisation of men, technology and material, more often than not such errors result from the lack of attempts at making technical decisions. Decisions appertaining to the use and coordination of the elements of the tool process are frequently made in terms of some traditional divination process which might have had some relationship with the operation of the tool-process by mere chance.

Human behaviour is a combination of two component parts that stand in historical opposition to each other: *One*, a part of human behaviour is verifiable, the *other part* is mystical, and the essence of the former is embodied in tools, both physical and conceptual. The use of tools in the manner implicit in the tools themselves to produce verifiable results is termed technological behaviour. One aspect of this process that should be distinguished for clarity, is that one single tool can be used in the manner implicit in that tool for non-verifiable purposes, just as knives may be used as accoutrements of head-hunting. Such behaviour is governed by an overriding non-verifiable value judgment, because the purported supernatural efficacy of head-hunting is accepted on the basis of faith by the head-hunters, and it does not admit of being either proved or disproved. The locus of verifiable, technological, or instrumental behaviour is, therefore, in the directing process of valuation. Verifiable behaviour is perpetually self-correcting through its continual referent to the continuum of the past, the present, and the future, that is, the means-end-continuum.

The tools and patterns of tool using behaviour, that is, technology, apparent at any given time is the outcome of a process of evolution because new tools are the end result of unique combinations of the concepts embodied in previously existing tools, just as the automobile is a combination of several tool concepts. Tools are not only combined such that the nature of each tool is observed in the formation of a new tool, but the tools are also combined into interlocking patterns, where the individuality of each tool is preserved and the individuality of each tool contributes to the workability of the entire gamut of interdependent mechanism. Such a combination sometimes partakes the nature of a factory or a railroad. Additionally, these tool patterns are combined into a more extensive complex where the relationship between some of the parts of the unified network may be only indirect. The inter-relationships between parts of the industrial system, for example, is more clearly reflected in some instances, (for instance between agriculture and the steel industry) than it is in other (such as between petroleum and textile industry). The functioning of tools is not independent of men, as organizers, and goods and resources, as material. The functioning mechanism emanating from the integration and coordination of organisers and material, that is, of men, tools and materials, into a "well knit cob-web" of interdependent parts is rechristened as the "tool-process". The effectiveness of the tool-process is a function of two things: *one*, the efficiency of each of the interdependent parts that form the "cob-web", and *two*, the organization of the component elements in the "cob-web".

The task of integrating and coordinating the elements of the tool-process may be conceived of as being external to that process itself, which however is erroneous. The combination of tools for forming new tools or the combining of tools into interlocking patterns, the coordination of tools with men and materials, and use of tools and the verification of the effectiveness with which tools are used are all implicit in the structure of the tools themselves and is expressed through human beings, and human beings themselves are unique tools in the total tool complex, a fact that is becoming increasingly apparent with the strides made in realm of developing the number of inorganic tools to relieve human beings of not only particular aspects of human labour, but even certain functions hitherto performed by human brain as well.

However, there are hindrances in the way of the internally directed process of integration and coordination of the tool complex. Technology "is but one aspect of culture and that culture exhibits another aspect which is inhibitory to the technological process just as gravitation inhibits centrifugence."[17] The interrelationships between the tool-process and the inhibiting aspect of human behaviour are the sources of the problems with which economics is concerned with and the effectiveness with which the tool-process is coordinated is a function of the relative strength of the two forces. Thus "the history of the human race is that of a perpetual opposition of these forces, the dynamic force of technology continually making for change, and the static force of ceremony, status, mores, and legendary beliefs opposing changes".[2]

The life-process is supported by technological behaviour by seeking verifiable ends which, in turn, have verifiable consequences, but ceremonial behaviour leads to the diversion of tools into channels of use which are not self-correcting by verification through the experiential referent of the means-end continuum. Small wonder then, that the Neanderthal man for centuries buried his dead near the fireplace, apparently in the lasting belief that returning heat to the body would put like back into dead corpse. That the attempt never succeeded did not either cause dismay or result in changes in the experiment, nor was consideration given, to the consequences that would follow had the experiments at avoiding death been successful. The time dimension of the mechanism which provided food or the life space of the process which provided food, had the population continually increased owing to births, and never diminished by death, never entered into the calculations. Ceremonial behaviour is determined by tradition, superstition, or imagination, and the results of such behaviour are evidenced only in faith and emotion. Whether the purported end results of such behaviour were achieved or not, can be neither proved nor disproved because of the ceremonial behaviour: if rains follow a rain dance, the interrelationship between the dance and the rain is not verifiable.

Ceremonial behaviour in addition to resulting in human failure to use his tools most effectively possible, produces results that undermine human welfare. There are several adverse effects flowing from the behaviour patterns which admit of the possibility of the continued existence of the surplus problem, for example. Ceremonial behaviour is not verifiable in terms of demonstrable consequences, and therefore, the danger of injurious behaviour being there throughout eternity looms excessively large. The principal consequence of ceremonial behaviour is the perpetuation of the status relations which entwined the tool-process in the past, and therefore the surplus problem whose primary cause is embodied in certain patterns of non-verifiable behaviour, has a traceable history of five thousand years at least.

Functional Relationship Between Men & Tools

As the evolution of technology from the first general tools into a complex of specialized tools occurred, the coordination of men and tools into technological patterns generated a spectrum of functional relationship between men and tools. The development of cultural patterns where some tools were used by only a portion of society, that is, of specialization of labour, produced a set of technical relations between men, *inter se*, based upon their technical relations to the specialized tools. For example, in a complex tool pattern some individuals took decisions that affected others. However, at once, the ceremonial component of the culture stream that pre-dates contemporary culture had a set of relations which imputed quality, formed the basis on which men were ranked in a superior-inferior status hierarchy. The chief was considered more important that the average hunter of farmer. The individuals who ranked high in the status hierarchy were allowed in society certain positions which continued in existence irrespective of changes in the individuals who were accorded the various roles. Once established, the relative prestige and status of a ceremonial position was imputed to whatever individual the society allowed to occupy the role, and as certain traditional methods were entrenched for selecting the individuals to occupy certain roles, it was believed that the rank of the individual in the status hierarchy was a function of the worth of the individual, and not of his importance or virtue derived from his being chosen to fill a certain position.

The individuals occupying status roles also have had certain technical relations to tools and to other individuals, which is why the various ceremonial positions occupied by men became traditionally associated with particular technical functions. The inherent virtue of man was thought of as having bearing on the status of the individual, and the technical position he filled was endowed with a corresponding relative importance. Concomitantly, the technical positions became infused with relative status ranks and the status hierarchy got superimposed upon the tool-process.

The status rank imputed to the various technical positions in the tool-process led to the conception that some positions were more important, or more productive, *vis-a-vis* others, which need not be true as can be seen by conceptualising a hypothetical technical process, where all the parts of the process are so interdependently related to each other that the malfunctioning of any one part would result in the malfunctioning of all other parts. The technical process of maintaining public health, involving amongst others, the department of sanitation, including the collectors of garbage, and medical services including doctors of preventive medicine, is a classic example in point. It is obvious in such a case that, technically, each of the parts is indispensable and of equal importance in the tool-process for one can not function optimally without the other so doing. Nevertheless, the technical positions were ranked in an ordered hierarchy, in accordance with an imputed relative importance, and the individuals filling the technical positions were conceived of as possessing varying amounts of technical value. This imputed value of the individual found expression in terms of degrees of skill and ability or amounts of productivity. Both individuals and technical positions were, thus, conceived of as embodying varying amounts of technical importance, when in reality imputed value was the transference of the concept of mystical status originally believed to be inherent in individuals to the tool process. The validation of status, in terms of imputed technical value, was an attempt at conferring on the ceremonial component of culture some of the certifiable attributes of the technological component.

> The belief in the substantial identity of rank with actual competency implies, and means to imply, that it was considerations of actual competency which in the first place led to the recognition of the distinction of rank. . . . The precise contrary happened is the case. The distinction of status

was established first, and it was thereafter assumed to coincide with possession actual technological competency.[3]

The super-imposition of the status hierarchy upon the tool-process is significant in so far as it inhibits the integration and coordination of men, technology, and materials. Effective organization of men technology and material, and a consequent reduction in the surplus problem, was possible by technical decisions made on a verifiable, experimental, self-correcting basis, but, decisions appertaining to the organization of the tool-process cannot be made exclusively on the basis of technical considerations, because of the inhibiting influence of the ceremonial component of culture.

The status positions were ranked in a superior-inferior hierarchy, therefore, and a natural presumption emerged that the individuals occupying the various status positions were superior or inferior *vis-a-vis* individuals of other ranks, in consequence of which customary patterns of reciprocal inter-relationships between the various ranks developed along lines which mirrored the relative status of the positions, and a whole cob-web of attitudes and symbols evolved about the various status positions: a way of life appropriate to each rank developed. The individual who occupied a particular position was supposed to possess certain accoutrements, and that individual's relationship with others were presumed to follow a given pattern. Every rank was indicated by a set of symbols of position, like a distinctive dwelling, a customary dress, exclusive food habits, and a certain deference in the manner of speech which incumbents in other ranks were to exhibit towards each other.

Perhaps while technology remained general and each family was primarily self-sufficient, the available goods were pooled and then allotted in appropriate amounts directly to each status position within the producing units, but the advent of specialized technology, caused the goods essential for providing each status position with the accepted symbols and requirements commensurate with each rank to be drawn from several different parts of the tool-process. The prerogative of status got invested in the occupants of the status positions in the hierarchy with varying amounts of power to command tribute from the other members of society. Because, each status position was associated with a particular technical function, and because rank was validated in terms of imputed technical importance, the various positions were endowed with authority by the rationalization of the postulates that the contribution of each individual occupying the status positions to the total effort of the society entitled him to an apportionment of the available goods in the proportion to the position be enjoyed under the then prevailing dispensation.

Status Power, Ownership and Value

The authority of status-power to command tribute then prevailing dispensation, flowed from the development of the concept of ownership. Technology, materials, and even people, came to be considered as property and private property at that, and the most important aspect of the patterns of status exemplification, then, was the command over people, technology, and materials, given the status positions in varying amounts, because, " . . . there is an intimate relationship between prestige and the control of economic resources in most societies."[40]

The authority to command tribute took many forms: exclusive rights to hunt in jungles and fish in waters, first fruits of trees, first to sow the fields, mandatory offerings and gifts, taxes and fines in kind, monopoly of trade in certain items, and tribute in the form of free labour to be used in building houses, tilling land, and fighting wars.

> Many instances of other kinds of intangibles, held as property by non-literate peoples, much as we hold patents and copyright, have been given. Bungel, in a brief passage, extends this by indicating that these rights form the basis of monopolistic production, and stresses their role in the establishment and maintenance of class and caste divisions.[5]

The concept of private property endowed the individuals who owned parts of the tool-process, with a claim to the goods produced from or with their property, and, even though these goods may not necessarily meet the requirements of their status position, the desired goods might be obtained in exchange for the goods on hand, which led to the problem of exchange, namely what quantity of one commodity should be exchanged for a unit of any other commodity offered for exchange, or, in modern terminology, how was the price or value of a commodity determined ?

Individuals comprehend by establishing relations. As a general rule measures begin with a defined amount and any actual amount is understood by its relationship with the *a priori* base. Commodities in the economic sense were no exceptions to this general rule. Because man devised a system of decision-making based upon equal exchange, (and not on some other method of deciding how the tool-process should be organized) it is necessary to relate goods to each other. Whereas this is achieved in primitive societies, by comparing amounts of the actual commodities themselves, it is done in other non-primitive societies by relating each commodity to some other given commodity, or representative yardstick, such as money, which becomes a measure of value or a common denominator of exchange, and that which raises the additional questions, however, about what is inherently ingrained in all commodities that is comparable, and given a value, what is inherently ingrained in all commodities which has a certain inter-relationship with other commodities *inter se* or with the common denominator of all commodity values. Value expresses the inter-relationship between commodities, but upon what characteristic of goods does value depend ?

Over past several centuries several price theories have been expounded, but they have failed to establish if there is any correlation either between value and any physical characteristic such as weight or volume, or between price and technical importance. Adam Smith,[6] David Ricardo,[7] and Karl Marx[8] failed in the determination of a means at effectively measuring relative amounts of embodied labour. Some economists like Stanley Jevons had a theory that took "utility" as the common denominator of value,[9] but the only proposed measure of this quality has been based upon an erroneous concept of individual psychology and, in any case, is not measurable since it differs for every individual and for the same individual at different times. The concept of supply and demand as determinants of value in the Marshallian sense like a pair of scissors cutting a price of cloth necessitates the prior acceptance of the traditional concept of utility. Marginal productivity cannot suffice without some hope of finding a way of measuring the relative productiveness of various commodities and, therefore, requires an answer to the problem of measuring embodied labour or utility. The cost-of-production theory also provides no answers of the question since it holds that the value of a commodity is a function of the values of other commodities that went into its production. At some point one has to accept that it is necessary to determine the value of a commodity from some other source, or rest with the thought that there exists no explanation of how the circle begins.

There exists possibly no instrumental determinant of the relationship between various commodities in terms of some quality that is common to all commodities. The only attribute that different goods and services could have in common, other than a possible but unmeasurable technical function, is some non-verifiable, mystical quality imputed to them by man. The failure of traditional concepts of price values to supply a complete answer to price behaviour was best illustrated by the problem identified by Arnold Toynbee in eighteenth century England that when real wages increased, unemployment increased simultaneously.[10]

Some exchange price relationship apparently fits the explanations of economic price theorists, but many do not. That goods are not exchanged on the basis of embodied labour is indicated, for example, by the relative values of the goods produced by highly mechanized industries and societies, with the goods produced by industries and societies that are less mechanised or more agarian: relatively small amounts of the former equilibrate for greater amounts of the latter. The concept of utility cannot explain things such as the extra length of the longest automobiles, that are prized primarily because they are not useful. Whereas some commodities exchange at prices several times their cost-of-production, the producers of others consider themselves fortunate when they manage to just recover their cost-of-production. Marginal productivity theorists cannot describe the process by which, at times, high values are placed on goods or services that serve to disrupt the productive process.[11]

There is nogainsaying the fact that the relationship between the price of any commodity and all other commodities must be explained in terms of some imputed quality that the goods have in common, but something has been left out from the equations of economic price theory. Toynbee's data illustrate this fact. Wages never plunge below a "floor" level, even in the face of widespread unemployment because competition and supply and demand operate to determine prices only within certain established and generally accepted limits. At times the socially accepted "floor" level may rise while at the same time the wisdom of economic price theory would have us believe that prices should be declining. The imputed quality that commodities have in common is embodied status, and it is only an analysis of this factor that can explain the price relations completely.

Status, Moral Virtue and Tribute

The individuals occupying the various status

positions had imputed to themselves not only an appropriate technical competency, but were believed to possess a proportionate amount of moral virtue as well.

> It is as though individual personality or force of character was a quantitative matter, a mystic potency capable of being reduced by infractions of taboo. . . .
> This mystic potency is also capable of being increased. We gain in more stature by scrupulous observance of the code and most particularly by "virtue" of ceremonial investiture, which is what the Polynesians call "mana". . . . More specifically "mana" is the mystic potency which is thereby increased. It is literally absorbed from contact with the virtuous who (and which) are thus also said to possess "mana". In ceremonial investiture "mana flows from the person of the shaman or from the sacred stone into the person of the chief".[12]

But, even in times as recent as the seventh century B.C., the Greeks attributed a similar mystic potency to things other than men. In fact, it is believed that it was at that time that man's concept of the essence of naturalistic phenomena underwent a change from pure "animism" to what may be termed "metaphysical".

> Homer and Hesiod, saw the "creation" of the earth out of the ocean, and filled every tree and brook with a god or nymph, but there is a sybtle change in the emphasis; the goods and nymphs of mythology were human persons writ large. The "gods" and "souls" of Thales were conceived,

> so it seems, as *part of the nature of the natural object* regarded as an organism.[13]

Imputation of mystical spirits to the natural world was not confined to the Greek culture, because, as Leslie White has emphasized:

> In the beginning of human history, man's philosophies were wholly animistic; he diffused his psyche throughout the cosmos; he confused the self with the not-self at almost every point.[14]

However, the fact of man's imputing a mystic potency to all things alone provides no answer to the question as to what is the measurable value which all commodities commonly possess which can form the basis of an exchange system. Some insight is gained when we consider that in

> . . . all groups personal ownership of woke goods and rights exists. . . . Those things a man uses most constantly, those things of immediate importance to him as a means either to biological cervical or to *maintain his proper place in society*, become almost a part of him, both in his own mind and in that of his fellows.[15]

Thus the goods that were owned and exchanged by men, were deemed to possess the mystic potency of their owner, which was the value human being had imputed to all goods in varying amounts which like the mystic potency imputed to individuals, was a function of the status rank of the individuals who are owners of the goods. The mystic potency possessed by individuals admitted of incremental and decremental variations by ceremonial investiture or divestiture. Goods partook the nature of status symbols for designating ranks of individuals in the status hierarchy, while the goods themselves were endowed with different amounts of mystic potency. It almost naturally follows, therefore, that status could be invested or divested by the gain or loss of goods. Because goods came to be perceived as status symbols, individuals who owned goods could possibly part with a portion of their mystic potency, only in exchange for an equivalent amount of imputed status in return, that is, the loss of mystic potency occasioned by relinquishment of some goods, must be at least compensated by a gain in mystic potency of the alternative good. Thus the process of reciprocal exchange that evolved for the ceremonial distribution of the goods available to society among members of the society itself, embodied the process of equal exchange of status. The mechanics of exchanging goods came to be recognised as an equalizer of the loss and gain of status symbols and mystic potency among the parties to an exchange. The prices, which could equalize the loss and gain of status in every transaction and without disturbing the existing status structure, were to be deemed to be the correct prices. Such prices would be in equilibrium, which were the equilibrium embodied in all "automatic" price structures: competitive, monopolistic, or otherwise.

Status was the common denominator of the exchange process, and therefore, the goods of an individual occupying a high position embodied more value than did the goods of those individuals occupying lower positions. Assuming that the institutional behaviour of extinct non-literate peoples gives indications of the early periods of civilization, one can seemingly maintain that the ratios at which goods were exchanged between people, were at the first instance determined by haggling in the market and were later crystallized (at least within a narrow range) by cultural values. The ratios of exchange agreed to between the parties were to an exchange dependent upon the relative status position of the parties to the exchange, and were determined by beliefs about the amount of status value the transfer bestowed or expended.

Economic theory enjoining that the process of exchange increases the utility of both parties to the exchange is correct in principle. People seek for their own use, and value greatly, the goods that are customary for their status position. Through exchange, both parties have command over the goods society has ordained for their possession.

The *ratios* at which goods exchange, particularly in non-industrialized societies, can be understood as well in terms of the process of maintaining status reciprocity in the social framework. The high status positions are validated by large amounts of a variety of goods, which must be secured from the many people who produce them, and therefore, the goods and authority available to the high status groups must secure in exchange quantum of the goods of others that was larger proportionately, for only then can the existing power status structure be perpetuated. When individuals of the high status groups do not receive sufficient tribute from others in terms of goods, to maintain their position in the power-status hierarchy, or when relatively low status groups receive too much goods and accumulate goods that are not customarily commensurate with their rank, the real problems arise.

The advent of money in the economic horizon, caused the common denominator of the exchange process, namely, status, to be reduced to units of money, which was received in payment for goods and services, and with which the goods and services of others could be purchased, so much so that the distribution of money was the distribution of purchasing power, that is, of command over men, technology, and materials. When goods were replaced by money as income, the various status positions in the social framework were accorded different amounts of incomes approximately commensurate with the rank of the relative positions in the power status hierarchy.

The distribution of income, it is maintained, is a function of productivity, namely, of the contribution of the producing units to the aggregate produce of the society as a whole. This concept clearly imputes a relative status value to the functions of the technical positions of the tool-process and to the results of their efforts. Relative productivity cannot be compared in terms of any other common denominator. Income and imputed productivity, therefore, both depend upon status rank. Income is the tribute paid to the status position by the society.

The set patterns of tribute, or status, or investiture is not static in the sense that it gets disrupted over time as some individuals come to hold command over greater amounts of men, technology and materials, or as the technical relations of men are altered by the advent of new technology. A culture characterized by a status hierarchy, will have individuals attempting at obtaining as much of command over resources as possible for the things they offer in exchange, and part with as little as possible for what they obtain from others. In consequence, authority to dictate the use (or nonuse) of men, technology, and materials may at times allow individuals to demand and obtain such a high price for the goods they offer in exchange, that changes are affected in the established[16] flow of tribute, and such occurrences are not very rare, in a long history of attempts by society at controlling maximum and minimum prices. The first instance of such an attempt by society in recorded history, perhaps was the maximum prices and wages included in the Code of Hammurabi,[17] and subsequent similar attempts had been made with theories of "just" or "equilibrium" prices that set forth the conditions which must be satisfied for maintaining status reciprocity, and not force deviations from the existing status structure.

Equilibrium of the existing power-status structure is not always maintainable. Status differentials are maintained by the flow of tribute from the lower to the higher positions in the power-status structure. The process of equal exchange is one of tribute payments provided by the ratios of exchange together with reciprocal status exchange, for the maintenance of the existing power status pattern in our social framework. The emergence of new technology materially alters the set pattern of technical relations and whoever gains the property rights, over the new tools, men and materials, is able to command new tribute payments. The new or changing tribute payments clearly alters the system of power status equilibrium in the social framework, by closing incremental variations in the tribute received by some members of society and decremental variations in the tribute received by some other members, or alternatively, by establishing new status positions where none existed previously.

The disorganization of the power-status hierarchy of feudalism and the transition to that of contemporaneous pecuniary societies was conceived of by Adam Smith and his sucessors-in-calling as having a certain inter-relationship with the productivity process. The fertile imagination of the Scotch Philosopher and other economists in Britain, imputed to the scurrying status seekers a technical function. The function of the system of markets and prices, was confused with that of the tool-process, and despite the two being dedicated to conflicting tasks, the productive process was seemingly benevolently organized by the market system. The rationalistic philosophers reposed their faith in the Natural Order Phenomenon and held that Natural Laws operated to produce the greatest output of goods and services, and effected the most equitable distribution of the product, and this process was so ordained and carried out by the automatic action of the mechanism of markets and prices. Such a way of thinking has been perpetuated in the two preposterous assumptions: *one*, that prices measure technical productivity and *two*, that equilibrium prices and incomes lead to maximum technical efficiency. Equilibrium prices equalize the investiture or divestiture of status in society, which has prevented the development of more effective programmes designed, to ensure that the way is open for eventual restoration of property rights and power-status and the normal functional mechanics of the economy.

While the life-process of man is a function of the tool-process, society has undertaken a deliberate widespread effort to reduce the inhibitiveness of the ceremonial behaviour that dislocates the effectiveness of the tool-process, only in isolated instances.

Surplus and Non-Verifiable Beliefs

In economies characterized by a less specialized technology, the non-verifiable beliefs and traditions caused the emergence of a surplus problem that was much more important to the total society than it is in modern industrialized economies. Economies with less specialised technology did not produce the severe variations in the welfare of individuals, within the society, that are apparent today.

> These smaller groups may live on a level but little removed from subsistence needs, where the margin between starvation and survival is slight. Yet even in such societies, the individual who, as an individual, is reduced to such straits that he must either depend on some agency set up for the purpose of preventing his giving way before the harsh dictate of the economic system, or starve, is rarely, if ever, encountered.[18]

This variation in degree is attributed to two facts. *One*, the surplus problem is not as acute in terms of individuals as differentiated from the total economy, in non-literate societies, because none in such societies goes without any tool and material whatsoever. In any event sufficient tools can be constructed out of the given resources, by most members of the society and land was usually obtainable by mere appropriation *per se*, but this does not imply that the surplus problem originated with the advent of advanced technology. From a broad study of technology it has been concluded that

> . . . Although the existence of a simple technology makes the problem of survival acute, there is still no human group that exploits to the fullest its environment, even within the competence of its technological equipment.[19]

Two, the severity of the surplus problem in industrialized societies, is attributable to the price system.

> The relationship between the machine technology and the pecuniary organization of our economy has by no means been made clear. Yet it is apparent that this relationship has given rise to certain special kinds of economic phenomena, such as the business cycle, and the periodic unemployment that has followed on technological advance. These phenomena are the direct result of the increased productivity of the machine, coupled with a system whereby the sale of goods for profit as a technique for amassing wealth has become an end rather than a means in life. This entire complex operates so as to deprive many persons of an opportunity to obtain the basic necessities of living, no matter now willing they may be to work or how able.[20]

Surplus and Technological Advancement

The security of society has increased with the development of advanced technology, but the surplus problem has persisted and has resulted in limiting the effectiveness of the tool-process in solving the problems of society, particularly so, the problems of a particular section of society. Failure to coordinate properly the elements of the tool-process, (namely men, materials and technology) has in part, been caused by:

(i) the production of spurious goods that cannot partake the means for further production;
(ii) from the production of goods that are low in priority for the functioning of the tool-process *vis-a-vis* alternative goods;
(iii) from the use of insufficient skills in the organization of the tool-process due to status considerations;
(iv) from competitive salesmanship in the form of advertising as distinct from technical information, and unnecessary duplication of effort;
(v) from exploitative and wasteful use and recovery of materials;
(vi) from the use of obsolete technology; and
(vii) from what Veblen had called "conspicuous consumption."

Ineffective coordination of men, material and technology has led to :

(i) the production of goods that serve only reflect prestige or what we may call prestige goods;
(ii) the production of goods that serve as inferior means to further production; and
(iii) the failure to produce as much, as quickly, and as efficiently, as the elements of the tool-process could have produced had they been organized on the basis of technical considerations, and not on considerations of status hierarchy.

The ineffective coordination of men, technology, and materials is damaging, but the failure to integrate all of the elements of the tool process that are available is far more damaging. The tool-process is an evolving technological complex, and all points in this continuous organization of activity are amenable to viewing from the perspective of either the past, or the current, or the future patterns of activities. According as the point of view that is adopted, any technical activity which forms a constituent element of the problem-solving continuum is seemingly a process of production, distribution, or consumption. For example, when food is consumed the act of consumption is obvious; and apparently food consumption is productive in that it provides the energy that allows human being to engage in further productive effort. What is less apparent is that it can also be viewed as a process of distribution because the energy embodied in the food is distributed into the tool process through the consumer.

However, a portion of the available elements of the tool-process may not be, either wholly or inpart, integrated into the tool-process, that is, they may not be used (either in part or wholly) as a constituent of the continuous productive effort, and a portion of the men, material and technology that are used may not be properly coordinated as effective parts of the tool-process. To the extent the elements of the tool-process are properly coordinated, they will be so organized that the goods that can serve as the most effective means for further productive effort are produced, but to the extent that the materials produced are not integrated and coordinated into the tool-process so as to become a means of further productive effort, it causes dislocation in the continuous process of production, distribution, and consumption. The use of a portion of the elements of the tool-process in a manner that eliminates them from the ongoing productive effort is a process of consumption only; it does not lead to further desired ends.

It is important to underscore here that leisure is a necessary part of the productive process, and as technology progresses, increasing amounts of leisure may be desirable.

The subjugation of the tool-process to the dictates of a status system which seeks to perpetuate itself is the major source of the surplus problem. The use of tools and materials by men, seeking to secure a livelihood, is a function of the decisions made on the basis of status authority. The high status groups in the power-status hierarchy of the social framework control most of the tools and materials available to society.

To obtain the authority to put them to use, the low status groups were required to part with a large portion of their (low status groups) output to those of high status in return. The high status groups would allow low status groups to use materials and tools for producing goods, as long as they desired additional commodities, as tribute, either for consumption or for accumulation in warehouses as marks of status rank. The grant of sanction by the high status groups, for the use of the elements of the tool-process, for productive purposes, to the low status groups followed a scheme of priorities. First, the peasants would receive such sanctions for agricultural produce, and then in addition to the peasants, some of the low status groups would be permitted to produce as artisans. Once the desire of the high status groups for tribute, in the form of produce both from agriculture and handicrafts could be satisfied, by the efforts of men who were smaller in number than the total population, the remainder of men were denied sanction to use technology and materials for producing goods. The surplus problem would be evidenced by men, excluded from the functioning economy, unused technology and materials, and surplus goods accumulating in warehouses.

With the flux of time new types of products would be discovered and desired by the high status groups, more workers would be required to produce the new commodities, a part of the surplus population would be absorbed into the functioning tool-process and the surplus problem would be relieved at best temporarily, till the new desires for tribute were being satisfied. The surplus problem would sometimes be reduced by the migration of a part of the members of the society to other areas, and when with the establishment of trade with new areas more or new goods became available to the high status groups, men, technology and material would be used in greater number to obtain commodities needed to exchange for the foreign goods.

In so far as the low status groups could retain more of their output than what they consumed they were in a position to exchange goods among themselves. Farmers with surplus goods which were not consumed, would not form the basis for more farmers, but more artisans could obtain food by producing goods to be exchanged for goods produced by the farmers. The integrated tool-process included both the low status groups necessary to provide the tribute desired by the high status groups, and those groups which were required to provide the goods they were allowed to exchange among themselves as well.

The number of farmers and artisans that could be supported by exchange of goods among themselves was inversely proportional to the portion of total output appropriated by the high status groups. With the increase in the amount of output retained by the low status groups, the tool-process expanded for the absorption of more men, technology, and materials. The quantum of men, technology and material kept out of the tool-process depended directly upon the concentration of status power and inversely upon the amount of total output retained by the low status groups. If, increased efficiency or new tools, caused a sudden burst in the output of the productive process, the quantum of the elements of the tool-process needed to provide the tribute desired by the high status groups may be diminished. In consequence a portion of the workers who had been integrated into the tool-process would be ejected and added to the surplus population, and additionally more technology and materials might also become surplus. The process of increasing efficiency or operationalisation of the new technology may result in the absorption of the tasks of certain workers, who would be added to the surplus population except in cases of individuals who would succeed in displacing someone else out of the latter's integrated position.

Surplus, Money and the Tribute Phenomenon

The advent of money modified the problem considerably. The desire of the high status groups for tribute, in the form of money, to be accumulated as evidence of rank was not limited, as was the case with regard to the desire for tribute in kind, which was why the high status groups allowed the organization of men, technology, and materials into a productive process to the extent that the money tribute was forthcoming. Additionally the low status groups exchanged goods with each other in so far as money was available with which to make payments of tribute to each other. The availability of money to the low status groups, determined the boundaries of the tool-process.

The low status groups obtained money in exchange for the goods they produced provided they could locate individuals who were willing to buy them, and the amount the low status group could sell among themselves was limited by the fact that a share of the money was received by the high status groups (as tribute) which was not returnable to the low status groups. Therefore, the ability of the low status group to pay tribute was limited, and a portion of the men, technology, and materials could not be absorbed into the tool-process.

With the flux of time the quantum of money increased. The ability of the low status group to pay tribute expanded to the extent of the new money that became available to them. In consequence, more of the elements of the tool-process (men, technology and materials) could be absorbed in the tool-process, which would be able to expand till the increased ability to pay tribute had been completely absorbed. However, the danger of the source from which the additional money was obtained being cut off always lurked around the corner and once the source from which additional money was obtained was cut off, a decline to the lower level of activity would be ensured and some of the men technology, and materials that had become integrated into the tool-process would again by rendered surplus. If subsequently the amount of money were again increased, the tool process would expand for the absorption of more of the men, material and technology till such time as the source of additional money was cut off once again. Continuous inter-period change is germane to what is called "market functions."

The power-status distributive system is clearly the most important source of the surplus problem yet it is not the only such inhibitory ceremonial element. Example of the manner in which other non-verifiable beliefs generated a problem of surplus, even of food are not infrequent. Hark these words:

> For the consumption even of this elementary necessity is found to be influenced, if not actually determined, by all manners of traditions of what is and what is not suitable for human nourishment. Taboos and quite irrational ideas holding that certain consumable products should not be eaten . . . are found among all people. . . . A proposal among ourselves to substitute the meat of a horse for that of a cow, or of a puppy for that of a lamb, would scarcely be entertained.[21]
>
> It would not be difficult to range the other forms of primary consumption goods and indicate how similar traditional values are factors of the first importance in shaping the economics of consumption.[22]

Inhibiting ceremonial behaviour was germane to the surplus problem, but this does not lead to any natural presumption that perfect integration and coordination of the tool process were achievable in the absence of either status considerations or other non-verifiable traditional beliefs. Technical errors and technical failures also fail to integrate and effectively coordinate men, technology and materials into the tool-process. The hallmarks of technical valuations, however, are their verifiability and self-correctiveness and not their embodiment in customs, traditions, and unquestionable institutionalized value systems. Exposing and seeking to eliminate inhibiting ceremonialism, for allowing technical decisions as to the effective integration and coordination of the tool-process is the problem area where economists can be of assistance. It is a scientific process of experimentally developing hypotheses that can be acted upon in such a manner so as to verify whether the revised organization of activities achieved (or not achieved) a desired demonstrable result.

The capability of improving through analysis, the way in which human behaviour is organized to meet the problematic situations which arise in the life process, distinguishes man from other forms of organic life. However, this does not imply that man, through the exercise of free will, introduces much different concepts that previous knowledge has no bearing on them, because no supernatural source is available to man from where thoughts can be derived. All human thoughts and behaviours must necessarily emanate from culture, that is, from the evidence documentated by, and thoughts and behaviour patterns bequeathed from, past generations by the present one, and which each individual learns from his exposure to society.

However, as culture is handed down from one generation to the other, it is not static, and each generation adds to the thoughts and behaviour patterns of previous generations. Individuals assimilate the culture of the society in which they live, and in the process, various combinations of the existing cultural elements are crystallized, which constitute new cultural elements, which is way by which culture is transformed temporally. Several of the dimensions of the process of cultural progress can be compared to the development of the physical universe. As George Harrison has beautifully put it, that bears repetition here:

> Physicists have found only three forces in the universe: electric, magnetic, and gravitational forces; and every push or pull we know is a combination of these. They hope, with unified field theories, to prove that these three kinds of force are really only manifestations of one elementary force, of which matter is another manifestation. In any case, we know that matter is introconvertible with energy, . . . and that matter is itself composed of three basic particles: protons, neutrons, and electrons.
>
> From the three fundamental participles have been formed nearly a hundred kinds of atoms . . . These atoms in turn combine into several hundred thousand kinds of molecules, which further associate to form the millions of objects we can see.[23]

One of the distinguishing features of the aggregate of protons, neutrons, and electrons is to form themselves into an endless series of new combinations and produce unique forms of mass and energy. An individual particle might have no tendency to cooperate to form a complex combinations of particles, but a tendency of the formation of a complex combination of particles is a characteristic of the sum of the particles that are in proximity to each other. As Harrison wrote:

> Imagine a universe filled with particles of these three kinds flying higher and yon, exerting on each other the three basic, without direction or interrelation. This indeed would be choose . . .
> To build the universe as we know it, a directive force is needed. This may come from without, or may even be built into the nature of the particles themselves . . .[24]

Man is part of the particle, physical universe and, at once, of the cultural continuum. The physical processes involved in human existence and behaviour are dependent upon the physical universe, but what man does is a function of the cultural continuum. Culture consists of an aggregate of cultural elements, a portion of which, like the particles of the universe, tend continually to form themselves into new combinations and new cultural elements. Within the sum of culture is another part, ceremonials, which resist both change and new combinations because ceremonialism introduces a system of non-verifiable behaviour. The theory of cultural determinism is a statement of the fact that man directs the cultural continuum, no more than he directs the evolution of the physical universe. Culture is carried by man and can exist only in the presence of man, but the directing force of the continuum is embodied in culture itself, not in man.

Culture must be explained in terms of culture.

> Culture is a vast stream of tools, utensils, customs, beliefs that are constantly interacting with each other, creating new combinations and syntheses. . . . Man must be there, of course, to make the existence of the culture process possible. But the nature and behaviour of the process itself is self-determined.[25]

The effect of the development of knowledge and superior techniques on behaviour is neither denied nor is it maintained that man will not be better off as a result of such progress. Man will continue to behave as he learns to behave from his culture, but by and large the culture will produce verifiable behaviour which is not bound by past superstitions and non-verifiable values. The manner in which the development of knowledge influences behaviour is best illustrated in the words of John Dewey:

> Suppose, for example, that it be ascertained that a particular set of current coalitions have, as their antecedent historical conditions, the interest of a small groups of special class in maintaining certain exclusive privileges and advantages, and that this maintenance has the effect of limiting both the range of the desires of others and their capacity to actualize them. Is it not obvious that this knowledge of conditions and consequences would surely lead to revaluation of the desires and ends that had been assumed to be authoritative sources of valuation? . . . If, on the other hand, investigation shows that a given set of existing valuations, including the rules for their enforcement, be such as to release individual potentialities of desire and interest, and does so

> in a way that contributes to mutual reinforcement of the desires and interests of all members of a group, it is impossible for this knowledge not to serve as a bulwark of the particular set of valuations in question, and to induce intensified effort to sustain them in existence.[26]

The true significance of the concept of cultural determinism is that it reveals the necessity for careful studies of culture to serve as the basis for an understanding of human behaviour, "but", it should be pointed out with emphasis, this is not a philosophy of defeatism or hopelessness by any means. Least of all does it declare that one's efforts do not count. The fact that one's efforts to stamp out tuberculosis are culturally determined in no way minimizes the effort or the result.[27]

Several studies would be necessary to reveal the discrepancies between the status distribution of men, technology, and materials (that is the elements of the tool process) and the technical needs of the tool-process for integration and coordination. One part of the problem – namely, the integration of men and materials, is considered most important in the context of redefining economics as dealing with the problem of surplus.

Summary

Thus the real concern of the economists ought not to be the search of a system of matching limited (scarce) resources to unlimited wants. Economics is a study of the causes that leave uncoordinated the elements of the tool-process and is concerned with the effectiveness with which men, their tools and know-how, and the available materials are integrated and coordinated into a problem solving continuum, namely, a tool-process. Disclosure, and elimination, of inhibiting ceremonialism for allowing technical decisions as to the effective integration and coordination of the tool-process is the problem area which ought to be the domain of the economists.

NOTES

1. C.E. Ayres: *The Theory of Economic Progress*, (Chapel & Hill: The University of North Carolina Press) 1944, p. 121.
2. *Ibid.*, p. 176.
3. *Ibid.*, p. 160.
4. *Ibid.*, p. 390.
5. Melville J. Herskovits, *Economic Anthropology*, (New York : Alfred A. Knopf) 1952, p. 38.
6. See Adam Smith : *An Enquiry into the Nature and Causes of Wealth Nations*, 1776, reprinted and edited by R.H. Compbell and A.S. Skinner, with W.B. Todd as textual editor (Oxford : The Clarendon Press) 1976 in 2 volumes. And G.P. O'Driscoll Jr. (ed.): *Adam Smith and Modern Political Economy* (Ames, Iowa: The Iowa State University Press) 1979.
7. See P. Sraffa (ed). : *The Works & Correspondence of David Ricardo* (11 Volumes) (Cambridge: Cambridge University Press) 1951 - 1973. Mark Blaugh: *Economic History and the History of Economics* (Sussex: Wheatsheaf Books Let.) 1986 Chapters 4 and 5. See also G.A. Caravale and D.A. Tosato : *Ricardo and the Theory of Value Distribution and Growth* (London & Boston: Routeledge & Kegan Paul Ltd.) 1980, p. 4.
8. See Paul M. Sweezy : *The Theory of Capitalist Development : Principle of Marxian Politican Economy* (New York : Oxford University Press) 1942.
9. See George J. Stigler : "The Development of Utility Theory", in E. J. Hamilton, A. Rees and Harry G. Johnson (eds.): *Landmarks in Political Economy* (Chicago: University of Chicago Press) 1962. See also Amitava Mukherjee : *The Economic Theory of Human Resources* (New-Delhi: Indus Publishing Company) 1990.

10. Arnold Toynbee, *The Lectures on the Industrial Revolution of the 18th Century England* (London : Ravingstons) 1887, p. 100.
11. See Lester Thurow: *Generating Inequality* (London : MacMillan Press) 1975, pp. 211-230 and Mark Blaugh: The Methodology of Economics (Cambridge: Cambridge University Press) 1985, pp. 193-201.
12. Arnold Toynbee : *Op cit.*, p. 165.
13. *Op. cit.*, p. 11.
14. Leslie White, *The Science of Culture*, (New York : Farrar, Strauss & Co.) 1949, p. 66.
15. *Op.cit.*, pp. 372 and 380. Italics added.
16. Hammurabi's code consists of a compilation of older Akkadin and Sumerian Laws and tends to strike a balance between the two legal systems. He considered himself the "King of Equity " Law. See "Cuneiform Law", by Paul Koschakar, in *Encyclopaedia of Social Sciences* (New York : MacMillan Co.) 1954.
17. John Kenneth Galbraith, *A Theory of Price Control*, (Cambridge, Mass.: Harvard University Press) 1952, pp. 29-30.
18. *Op. cit.*, p. 31.
19. *Ibid.*, p. 271.
20. *Ibid.*, pp. 30-31.
21. *Op.cit.*, p. 271.
22. *Ibid.*, p. 274.
23. George R. Harrison, "Faith and the Scientist," delivered in 1953 as the Stearns Lecture at Phillips Academy, Ardover and published in *The Atlantic Monthly*, December 1953.
24. *Ibid.*
25. *Op. cit.*, pp. 339-340.
26. *Op. cit.*, pp. 49-60.
27. *Op. cit.*, p. 353.

4

A PROPOSAL FOR FUTURE POLICY

Pattern of Property Ownership

The present society was born out of the cultural heritage of the, generations that are no more, and modern men have received most of its people and culture from societies that have existed in the past almost throughout eternity. The culture of the present, nevertheless, is not a mere extension of other societies, because there exists today an unique cultural configuration peculiar to our times' social order. The isolation provided by the oceans and the fact that elements were borrowed from many societics which thrived in the past, to be combined into our culture indeed have, produced a break with some of the institutions of the past cultures.

We take great pride in the relative social equality of our culture: the division into castes is universally disapproved with a few exceptions, no citizen is mandated to kneel down before another or is required to avoid showing his back, yet with all its equality, the most satisfying characteristic of our society to most of its members remains to be the attribute of almost everyone being, at least able to hope to better his power-status position in the social framework. Our society, therefore, like the past cultures from which it was born and in which it has been nurtured, is burdened with a hierarchy of power-status positions. The power-status hierarchy of society is superimposed upon the tool-process, and technical decisions appertaining to coordination of the elements of the tool-process are made in terms of status considerations, and, therefore, failure to integrate and fully coordinate all the available men, technology, and materials has precipitated a surplus problem.

The now obtaining power status structure of our social framework has been considerably more fluid (downwards as well as upwards) than the power status patterns of most previous societies. Throughout most of the history of man, technology advanced so rapidly and had imposed such a disrupting impact, on a continuous basis, upon the power-status structure of contemporaneous society, that the identification of relative power-status positions, on a permanent basis, by reference to the technical positions of the tool-process with which they were associated, was impossible. Some individuals succeeded in rising to higher-status positions through the ownership of property rights over new technical functions, while others were destined to be pinned down to a lower status rank.

In the more stable societies that existed in the past, exaction of tribute was by rights over a given status rank, but as new technical positions developed, new status positions were created and the relative status rank of the new positions was often re-determined by the ability of the owners of the new technology to demand tribute. Not infrequently, therefore, status was obtained by command over tribute, and rarely discrepancies between the imputed technical importance of certain positions and their power to command tribute resulted in the generation of problems which was also a result of change.

As disintegration of tribal society set in under the weight of advancing technology, and the transference of the right to command tribute from personal relations and legally attached dimension to elements of the tool-process by property laws took place, the stage was set for a period of status mobility. The advent of money as the common denominator-measuring power of status position in the hierarchy, caused further diminution of the level of direct inter-relationship between status and personal relations. The right of those occupying higher position in the power-status hierarchy, to command tribute became synonymous with property rights, and property rights, in turn, were superimposed upon not merely all elements of the tool-process, but at once upon the ceremonial elements as well. The quantum of tribute appropriate to given property rights was not always determinable by custom, usage and practice, as the quantum of tribute appropriate to property rights was sometimes determined by the ability of others to pay tributes and the ability of the receiver to ward off competing demanders of tribute.

If the pattern of property ownership position which formed the basis of demands for tribute by those placed high in the power-status hierarchy was crucial to others in the power-status hierarchy as a status-symbol, or as a means for the latter to create additional property rights upon which to build their own tribute demands, a high tribute was likely to be forthcoming. The smaller the number of individuals controlling the property ownership rights attendant upon any technical function, the higher was the demands for tribute likely to be, because it was relatively a whole lot more easier to execute threats to withhold the use of the ownership authority. A higher availability of alternative goods or functions owned by others, had the effect of reducing the power to command tribute, and as Galbraith demonstrated,[1] the power-status position and the offsetting tribute commanding power of those from whom tribute was demanded affected the power to command tribute.

Our social status structure has become increasingly inflexible over the last two hundred years or so. The increasing scarcity of land which provides space for the surplus population to spread, and the control of property rights over more and more new technology by the existing occupants of the high power-status position, tended to crystallize the power-status hierarchy. The use of accumulated tribute for developing new technology, or for purchasing command over technology, provided protection to the relative positions of those occupying positions which were high in the power-status hierarchy of society. Elimination of competitions as frequently as possible and combination of property rights for increasing the power of each occupant of the power-status hierarchy to command tribute, were also deployed as a means to the establishment, and the maintenance, of relative positions in the hierarchy.

As crystallisation of the power-status structure got firmly entrenched and command over the tool-process got concentrated in fewer hands, the magnitude of the surplus problem vastly expanded, a fact that has not been fully revealed since the advent of the Second World War. During phases of expansion, the middle income groups expanded on account of the advancement of those in the lower rung of the power-status hierarchy to higher levels in status, but during periods of contraction the ranks of the poor got replenished. Advancement of those in the lower rungs of the power-status hierarchy to the middle income group did not bring forth permanent authority over technology, and when the market system no longer had the support of the expansion of the authority, obtained during the period of expansion, authority to hold command over technology will stand withdrawn in many cases.

Without effective efforts at alleviating the surplus problem, the prospect for the future is that it will become increasingly bleak. The rapid advancements in natural sciences, and electronics will soon provide instruments and machines to perform many of the tasks now laboriously performed by men. Not only would automatic firms and factories become common place, offices will increasingly be staffed, not by men, but by machines. By deploying all the technology available, it was estimated, sometime back, that United Kingdom, could concurrently increase output, and at once reduce the "work week" to a bare one hour per week. Granted that, a comparable situation is possible elsewhere as well. With successively morc advanced technology pressed into operation human efforts could possibly be redirected to far more productive and far more enjoyable pursuits for, or alternatively, more men could possibly be added continuously to the surplus population. The last alternative will prevail unless the surplus problem is adequately attacked by making the institutional pattern more responsive to the re-absorption and redirection of consequences emanating from human productive efforts.

The increasingly critical nature of the surplus problem emanating from the failure to reabsorb men whose tasks have been taken over by machines, made possible by the advancement of technology, might be offset, at least partially, by the decentralisation of industry. The use of the solar energy as fuel in automated firms and factories churning out several goods from a restricted group of materials through atomic reorganization could cause considerable decentralization of industry. Small wonder then that Wiener wrote -

> "We are now in a position to return to cottage industry, in places where it would otherwise be suitable."[2]

However, decentralization of industry without decentralization of power-status authority in society over the tool-process would, in all likelihood, redistribute the surplus population and not reduce it even marginally.

To reduce the non-integration of men, technology, and materials into the tool-process, efforts at altering the system of controlling the tool-process by status authority has to be resorted to in some form. All cultures are integrated to some extent and all cultures are in a state of disintegration to the extent that technological progress is disrupting the existing arrangement and, therefore, any proposal to circumvent the surplus problem must be at a rate of change that would not bring forth an intolerable disintegration of society. If, in the ultimate analysis, a solution to the surplus problem is to substitute technical decisions for status control over the tool-process, it must be achieved through intermediate ends-in-view. To say that the surplus problem grew out of ceremonialism, or to assert that the status distributive system is the primary cause of most aspects of the problem, is not enough, because devising a succession of ends-in-view which admittedly, do not obviate the problem, but which at once holds out the hope of evolving into further ends-in-view leading in that direction, is absolutely essential.

Analyses of the surplus problem that have served in the past as the basis for policy proposals offer little hope, if any, for the future. Programmes designed to raise prices, restrict output, or equalize misery are not likely to produce more effective integration and coordination of the elements of the tool-process. The men, technology, and materials allowed to be integrated by the status distributive system are circumscribed by the desires of those who occupy positions in the high status groups, for more goods and by the ability of the low status groups to meet the demands of those in the higher status group for tribute. Traditional proposals for solving the surplus problem have approached at the matter from the perspective of production adjustment, which has largely been ineffective in eliminating hardship and has, in fact, tended to excerbate the magnitude of the surpluses. Greater success might have flowed from an approach which attempts at optimally distributing what can be produced, rather than one which acts the other way around: that which seeks to produce what is distributable. If attempts are made at increasing production and consumption, rather than at adjusting production to the market, a better and more effective organization or coordination of the elements of the tool-process may have been achieved.

An anticipation of what would be required to satisfy many of the needs which individuals will experience in future is quite possible, and indeed, demand estimation by economists, econometricians and planners is quite common. Society could nearly succeed in satisfying these requirements much better than it has been able to do so in the past, but the productive process is not so organized and such decisions are erroneously made in terms of the dictates handed down by the system of markets and prices. Goods and services are distributed by prices on the basis of incomes, which is where the true problem lies. Can every individual be provided with the quantities of income required to enable the individuals to buy as much of the goods and services they want or need to buy, as society can produce and if yes how? Is it possible to alter the income system of distribution as to provide the most effective distribution of the goods and services society can produce, rather than limiting the output of society because some individuals do not have the requisite purchasing power? Herein lies the basis of the surplus problem and these are the primary questions which the free world must face in an awakening world, which is increasingly less tolerant of waste, inefficiency, misery and surpluses.

The quandary of capitalism can perhaps be best illustrated with the problem of distributing medical services. Estimation of the number of individuals in each age bracket who will suffer impairments to their health from various causes in a given period of time is possible with considerable accuracy. Society could provide the hospitals, medicines, equipment, and men required to take care of that magnitude of health problems, but capitalistic societies distribute these medical goods and services on the basis of income, where it is known that the requisite income might not be available with the individuals. Thus, the basic question that remains unsolved is how to provide the requisite income necessary for purchasing the requisite medical care. An already difficult problem is further complicated by the fact that despite the number of patients of various types being estimable, it is nevertheless not possible to estimate which specific individuals will need medical service and what specific medical care at that, which explains why the question pertaining to who should receive the income with which to pay for that specific medical service, cannot be answered. The sick and the needy, who require specific medical care do not have the income with which to pay for it, which forces them to take recourse to charity, but the problem again is that enough charity is not available to save the thousands of individuals from suffering (including the individuals who are willing to suffer the stigma of living on charity to obtain relief). That unsatisfied demand for medical services exists, is just one of the several dimensions of the surplus problem because human suffering could be alleviated or avoided, by a better distribution of the medical services which society can currently produce.

For society to produce, it is arguable, the additional medical services which would be sufficient to meet all the needs arising from the health problem would necessitate curtailing the production of other goods and services which society values more highly, as evidenced by allocation of higher income for them, rather than for additional health services. Such an argument is implicit in the assumption that the system of markets and prices achieves the optimum allocation of productive effort, but the argument is fallacious because the individuals who need the additional medical care would spend the requisite income for its obtention provided they actually had the income to do so, and because society could produce the additional medical care without reducing its output of any other commodity. Indeed were it possible to coordinate more effectively the surplus men and materials with the most advanced technology potentially available, adequate provision for the much needed medical care, and the much needed food, clothing, housing, education, and many other goods and services could be produced in adequate quantities to greatly reduce the misery caused by the inability of many individuals to have access to them. This would warrant no cut in the amount of any commodity being enjoyed by other individuals, but it would result in more of everything being available even to such individuals who already consume the greatest amounts.

The surplus problem looks pretty much the same in the realm of agriculture as in medical services, and all activities that proposes to adjust output to the market in terms of an accepted "fair" price, serve to perpetuate the problem. It is possible to estimate how much food is needed to meet any socially accepted food consumption level measured in terms of calorie intake[3] or whatever else, and society can come much nearer to producing the requisite amount of food, than it has been able to do in the past, but the trouble is that the income necessary to purchase the appropriate quantity of food at a "fair" price would not be available with the individuals. The general conclusion that emerges, therefore, is that output should be adjusted to the market, which proposal does precious little to solve the surplus problem.

The underlying assumption that output should be adjusted to the market is based on the basic premise that the desired ends of productive process can be determined by society only through the allocation of income, and, further, that there exists no other means which could ensure each individual of his "fair" share of that part of the produce of the economy which he is interested in receiving. The share of aggregate output due to each individual has been defined as that amount which his income will purchase because each individual is assumed to receive purchasing power in exact proportion to the worth of his contribution to the output of the total society. Various aspects of this theory are vulnerable and hence open to serious questioning, which we discuss below.

Individual Entitlements

In what respect is each individual "entitled" to a share of the total output of the economy based upon his contribution to that produce? Do the free economies actually wish to allocate the aggregate produce of society on the basis of individual contributions thereto? Certain groups, such as children, the disabled and the aged, are expected to receive a greater share of the total output of society than they are considered capable to producing, and the contribution to total output of some individuals is assumed to exceed their desire, or will, to consume goods and services which they produce.[4] Shall we say then that the difference between the amount of output attributed to, and the amount of output consumed by, such individuals should be either allowed to be wasted or be added to the store of surplus goods, and, therefore, removed from the ongoing productive process? If there are individuals who have both the desire and the ability to be more effectively coordinated into the tool-process, and if individuals wish to contribute more to total output of the economy, irrespective of the way in which society purports to measure contributions, but is prevented from so doing, is there any justification for determining their individual "fair" share on the basis of their respective current contribution?

In real life conditions such measures of worth, or contribution, to the total output of society, by individuals is a function of the imputed power status and probably without any consistent inter-relationship whatsoever to the effective functioning of the tool-process, and questions appertaining to "fairness" can be given verifiable answers only in terms of the ends-mean continuum of the tool-process. What is "fair" or proper for the individual should be judged on the touchstone of, not some traditional non-verifiable ideal, but of its consequences for the individual and for the society in its entirety.

This then raises the additional set of questions. Is income distribution amongst individuals based on the foundation of the contributions of the respective individuals to the total output of the economy? If the measures were recast in terms of productive effort, it might be possible to hold that such effort could be measured in terms of some alternative yardstick such as hours of work, but even that does not carry us very far since difficulties would still persist, as Adam Smith, David Ricardo, and Karl Marx had discovered,[5] on account of the fact that society imputes higher value to some effort than to others and some tasks are considered less irksome than others. When the problem relates to determination of a specified identifiable portion of aggregate output of society attributable to a given individual, the difficulties increase several folds, particularly so, in highly complex economies criss-crossed by diverse indirect inter-relationship between the myriad parts of the total tool-process. In fine, there is then no way of measuring technical contributions of individuals to the aggregate output of society. In chapter 3, an attempt was made to show that there exists no way of equating goods or output in terms of any technical quality held in common by all such goods, but such a common denominator can, and is, imputed to goods. Western society and its Eastern precursors imputed a status-power to all goods, which is the common denominator in terms of which quantities are evaluated.

Thus, in a capitalistic system of social organisation, distribution of goods is governed by incomes, and incomes are distributed on the basis of the relations of imputed status. That distribution of income is effected on the basis of traditional power-status considerations and not in proportion to individual's contributions to aggregate output of society, is palpable from the fact that the best way to obtain a higher income is often seen as inherent in obstructing the full operation of the tool-process, rather than to produce more. The distribution of goods, based on income has caused a surplus problem because some individuals do not wish to spend all of their income for the goods that are produced, (or what may be called by some as "under consumption") while other individuals who desire the goods, do not have the income to pay for them. Production is, therefore, determined by the effective market, and the surplus problem largely results, from a distributive system based upon a rationalisation that is not verifiable.

An economic system where production is adjusted to the market, characterises capitalism. If this characteristic of capitalism is an aspect of the system prized so highly by most developed countries, and if this is the focal point of the current ideological controversy, particularly in Eastern Europe, the capitalistic nations are in the none too comfortable position of seeking to perpetuate the surplus problem in any eventuality. The question is whether the developed countries can reverse the system of adjusting production to market, adhered to for over past several thousand years, and adjust the market to output, while at once leaving unimpaired the cultural elements that make the system more democratic and, hence, superior to alternative systems. It is to be hoped that greater importance will be attached to solving the surplus problem than to maintain the income distributive system in its present incarnation without further change. The critical question that remains to be answered is whether determination of output in terms of technical decisions regarding the coordination of the tool-process is possible, and then whether determination of how the market can be organised to effectively distribute that amount of total produce of society is possible, which in turn involves the resolution of two fundamental issues: *one*, do the developed nations insist that the pattern of distribution of aggregate output of the economy has to be worked out on the basis of individual incomes, and *two*, is it possible to develop such a system of democratic distribution grounded in income allocation which does not embody the surplus problem ? For example, can the distributive system be so improved as to make possible the distribution of as much food and medical services as can be produced to relieve the existing misery meted out to some individuals as they fail to obtain as much food and medical service as they need or demand?

Free societies have been the subject of criticism for answering the first question in the affirmative, and for failing to forcefully seek an affirmative answer to the second one. A concerted effort to improve the distributive system so that the market can be adjusted to output, instead of adjusting production to market, must be forthcoming soon if the developed economies are to succeed in furthering the development of democratic societies.

Progress towards making the income system of distribution work in a manner designed to reduce the surplus problem, rather than to perpetuate it, is possible provided, as an initial end-in-view, the level of normal operation of the tool-process can be raised, and fluctuations in the ability of the market system to distribute the goods that are produced are avoidable. In case the economy could be stabilized at the level of moderate prosperity, greater participation of the non-integrated portions of the available men, material and technology would be allowed in the functioning of the tool-process, and poverty would be reduced substantially.

Markets and Purchasing Power

In modern monetized economies, output of the productive process is often distributed through the system of markets and prices by the transference of money or credit. Goods, then, are distributed on the basis of income or purchasing power, and income or purchasing power being, in turn, distributed more or less on the basis of the hierarchy of status positions, which is quite unequal. The ability of the system of markets and prices to distribute goods is a function of the availability of purchasing power in the hands of people who want the goods. The flow of purchasing power is such that in the process of producing goods, enough purchasing power to pay for buying the goods that are produced becomes potentially available, but a part of the purchasing power which becomes so available may pass on to individuals or combination of individuals who, because their incomes exceed their demand for goods, do not want to purchase the goods produced by society, that is, they resort to under-consumption, and concurrently, there may be others who want to buy the goods but do not receive sufficient purchasing power with which to pay for buying them. Once this occurs, the system of market and prices, will not be able to distribute all of the goods produced by society and there will be a surplus of goods and men. Despite the need for all the goods produced being in existence, and despite sufficient purchasing power being potentially available to individuals for making their purchase possible, the system of markets and prices may fail because the people who come to possess the purchasing power do not have the desire to buy the goods produced by society, and the people who have the desire to buy the goods, may have no purchasing power to do so.

There exists a floor or bottom line below which the market will not shrink, and the market shrinks because the status distributive system allocates more purchasing power to some individuals than they are able to spend, or they want to spend, but when all incomes have shrunk to the point at which every individual exhausts all of his incomes in buying the produce produced by society, or the failure of some individuals to spend all of their incomes in buying the produce is compensated by the tendency of others to spend more than they receive, the market can shrink no further. That is, modern monetized societies inherently attain stability only at the depth of depression. Any economy that employs the status distributive system will continually tend to move towards this floor level.

The total of all incomes received in any country each year is a multiple of the quantum of actual money (metal, paper, and check-book) in circulation, which means that on an average a unit of money is spent several times a year (our good old quantity theory of money), but when a unit of money received as income by an individual is not spent, the unit of money does not serve its normal function of appearing as several units of income during the year and therefore, in effect purchasing power has been destroyed or what may be called a "leakage" from the stream of purchasing power. A situation akin to this obtains in all cases where a country purchases goods (imports) from other countries which exceeds in value what it sells (exports) to them that is, when a country faces an adverse balance of trade. Moreover, most of the money in circulation in the developed countries or highly monetized economies are checkbook money, or plastic money (credit cards) both of which along with most paper money, are created and put into circulation only as banks advance credit. Banks in the act of creating credit, operating on the fractional reserve principle, create money.[6] When income is spent to liquidate a bank credit, the procedure by which the monies were created is reversed and money is destroyed. The monies can be created and put into circulation again only by another round of credit creation of equivalent magnitude. Either of these ways of destroying money causes the market to shrink to generate a surplus of goods.

The tendency of the market to shrink to the floor level and of purchasing power to be destroyed through either of the two channels discussed in the foregoing paragraph, can be offset if the banking system creates new money by creating credit for individuals who wish to buy goods and services, which additionally makes it possible to induce the market to rise above the floor level. If the economy has been operating at the floor level which exhausts all income in buying the goods produced by society, the expansion of credit and the distribution of new purchasing power to individuals who would expand it, will allow the use of additional amounts of men, technology, and materials to produce the goods they desire. The market will expand and will continue to expand till such time as creation of new purchasing power is not pre-empted and till such time as the new purchasing power so created is injected into the system for distribution to individuals who would expend it at a rate which "over-compensates" for the purchasing power that others destroy. There is, however, no presumption that the market will necessarily continue to expand only as long as the rate at which money is being created exceeds the rate at which money is being destroyed. If the process of new money being put into circulation is so regulated that they are expended more often, and, therefore, add more to total income, than the average money holding in the system, the market could continue to expand even where more money is being destroyed at a rate that exceeds the rate at which it is being created. If the new money that is spent less often than the average money holding, more money must be created to offset the impact of monies being destroyed, assuming that the money being destroyed have circulated at the average rate and no more, no less. If the money being destroyed have circulated at a rate, other than the average rate, the situation may not be changed materially, because the relative effect of the old and new money in creating purchasing power continues to determine the net change in market expansion or contraction.

The creation, distribution, and expending of new purchasing power can be caused by a wide variety of factors. War results in governments borrowing new purchasing power (deficit financing); industrial or geographic expansion induces private firms and individuals to borrow; usually to obtain command over the use of men, technology, and materials to be used in the production of more goods; rapid growth of population often leads to results that are similar to industrial or geographic expansion; a nation that exports goods of greater value than it imports (surplus in balance of trade) receives new purchasing power to make up the difference; governments may borrow new purchasing power in order to provide grants-in-aid; or loans to other countries (bilateral aid), or to carry out improvements within the country (financing economic development). The economic history of every country is punctuated with periods of credit expansion during which the market level was rising and the magnitude of surpluses was diminishing, which also demonstrates the effects of a fall in the rate of credit expansion and the resulting period of market shrinkage. Stabilization of the economy is possible at the level of prosperity only where new purchasing power could be created continuously at a rate which just offsets the purchasing power being destroyed, which might be accomplished if the government could continually borrow and distribute new purchasing power (money) at the required rate. The amount of new money essential for the maintenance of economic stability at a high level would vary continuously. The banking system will have to create new money and inject it into the system through credit creation at a rate sufficient to offset the effect of destruction of purchasing power through repayment of earlier credit, failures to spend income (under consumption), and possible unfavourable balance of trade.

Since credit creation would have to be a continuous process for replacing maturing loans and the purchasing power destroyed through alternative channels, the amount of credit outstanding would have to continually increase, but not all of credit created need be channeled to the government sector, because credit provided to the government sector has to have a logical basis. The amount of credit to be provided to government to offset the effect of destruction of purchasing power, will vary inversely in relation to the credit provided to private firms, individuals, and combination of individuals.

It is possible that the banking system at times may resort to credit creation at so rapid a rate that it results in the total purchasing power expanding more rapidly than the output of goods and services which creates an inflationary situation because (despite the continuing debate on the courses of inflation) the classic situation of "too few goods being chased by too much money" is arrived at. The nearer the economy approaches the conditions of "full employment" of existing plant capacity and the full absorption of the existing labour force, the more likely it is that such an inflationary situation becomes entrenched, because the possibility of increasing the output of goods becomes more unlikely. To avoid the adverse effects of inflation the government would have to cease borrowing and increase taxes above expenditures in order to mop up "disposable income" and destroy the excess purchasing power.

Achievement of economic stability by such a fiscal policy would be exceedingly difficult in actual practice, and the fact that the creation and destruction of money is controlled by banks does not reduce the difficulty. The banks, being themselves involved in the competition of tribute accumulation, inevitably must tend to magnify any expansion or contraction of the market. The expediency of good business dictates credit expansion when the market is expanding and to contract credit when the market is passing through the contraction phase, or when it appears that the market might contract in the foreseeable future. Thus, in addition to the normal action of the market system, the normal action of the monetary and banking system would have to be overcome by a fiscal policy designed to maintain economic stability. Since the controls of the government (unless the governments own the banks as in India) over the banking system are largely ineffective, it might not be possible for the government to avoid inflation by destroying money as rapidly as it is created by the banking system; and it might be extremely difficult, at times, for the government to create new money by borrowing as rapidly as the banking system and the status distributive system destroys it. Additionally, variations in the amount of currency held could at any time overcome all efforts of the Currency Creating Authority (Reserve Bank of India in India, the Bank of England in the U.K. and Federal Reserve System in the U.S.) to relax or tighten the credit and monetary system.

The psychological fall out and political problem that would be created by fear of an ever-rising public debt, and the financial problem of an ever-rising interest burden are added problems to be circumvented. A rising non-interest bearing national debt should theoretically arouse no fear, but a rising interest burden severely complicates matters. The low income groups are likely to own considerably less of the debt than the portion on which their taxes pay the interest, and, therefore, an inequitous redistribution of purchasing power from low to high income groups would ensue, which would increase the tendency of the market to fail to absorb all the goods being produced, because by and large it is the high, not the low, income groups, that withhold the spending of all of their income. Avoidance of this difficulty is possible if instead of resorting to availing credit, the government created it by simply requiring the banks to credit a special accounts with the required sum, which accounts could be classified as requiring no offsetting legal reserves and their use as legal reserves could be prohibited. They would constitute a new type of money to be added to the several types already in existence, and they need not be a disrupting influence upon existing money reserves. This is likely to undoubtedly face considerable opposition because much of the income of the banking system is derived from interest earned on credit created, and it would also fail to circumvent any of the other difficulties faced by a fiscal policy designed to stabilize the market.

If the creation and destruction of money were fully controlled by the government, new money could be created by maintaining whatever budget the legislature had set up, lowering taxes to reduce revenue, and making up the difference with newly created money (or deficit financing). The act of reducing taxes would, therefore, warrant the creation of new money, and new money would enter the market whenever taxes were lowered. If the taxes of the lowest taxable income groups were lowered, the new money would cause the greatest increase in total income and purchasing power in the system.

Bank credits established for itself by the government would not be credit *per se*, and hence there would be no interest burden and there would, therefore, be no fear that they might not be repaid. The accounts themselves would be legal tender, and the obligations of the government would increase little, if any, because the government stands behind the money system at present. Creating new money by means of a flexible tax system would allow the government to follow changes in the market more closely, and through experimentation gauging the amount of new money needed to offset observed tendencies of the market to shrink would be easy. The new money, created outside the credit creating mechanism, would not cause the outstanding debt to increase or the money destroyed by maturing loans. Such money would not by itself, therefore, increase the amount of new money required to maintain a stable market in the future.

If the development of new technology, or some other circumstances, induce a wave of unusual private borrowing (leading to credit creation) and spending, the tendency toward inflation could be contained by leaving the existing budget size untampered and by raising taxes.

With the increase in the physical output of the economy, the necessity of increasing the purchasing power in the market would emerge, which would contain any tendency of a downward pressure on prices. If the amount of money in the economy as production increases is not increased, it might cause temporary disruption of the traditional price relations, which could in its turn cause a period of price adjustments on a continuous basis and create some confusion in the market.

Where Are We Then

A programme for the maintenance of economic stability, such as the foregoing, at full employment of the population by controlled credit expansion would not eliminate altogether the surplus problem for that would be just one step in the right direction. Control of the tool-process would continue to be exercised in terms of status considerations, and integration of all the available population would not set right either the problem posed by non-integrated technology and materials, or by the problem of ineffective coordination of the elements of the tool-process, viz., of men, technology, and materials. A part of the population, would continue to receive fewer goods than what the society considers necessary for a standard of living that meets the minimum requirements of health and decency standard but to stabilize the economy at a relatively high level of operation would prepare the ground for improvements in the organisation of the tool-process continuously. Without the expectations of a future market failure, there would be the added inducement of continually increasing profits by not restricting, but increasing output. Distribution would be adjusted a good deal, to production rather than production being adjusted to distribution. The fact that more production of goods would have to be attained by more effective coordination of the elements of the tool-process and by integration of more technology and materials, leads us to the inference that there would be a tendency to reduce the magnitude of the surplus problem continuously.

Consumer education would become increasingly important. If full employment were assured and production were not deliberately curtailed to adjust to a shrinking market, the quantum and class of goods produced would be determined, by and large, according to the desires, to have goods, of income receivers. Therefore, the coordination of the tool-process admits of improvement by more intelligent buying on the part of consumers.

The tool-process operates only as tribute is paid, and, therefore, control over the tool-process by technical decisions could be affected only where it was possible to distribute purchasing power to individuals so as to coincide with technical decisions. Since achievement of full control over the tool-process by technical decisions is not possible, so long as control is exercised through tribute considerations, it may be necessary, with credit problem areas becoming more critical, to remove some technical functions from the domination of power-status authority. For example, with society sufficiently distressed by human suffering and loss of life owing to insufficient medical care in individual cases, distribution of medical care may be necessary on an alternative basis, and not on the basis of income of those who need medical services. Such a solution to particular problems could be particularly effective in all cases where meeting all the needs and desires of the entire population for the good or service is easy. With the tool-process becoming more effectively organized and new technology put into use, meeting the desires of all the people for more and more products will become a distinct possibility.

The proposals outlined here, if acted upon, would cause an increase in the amount of deliberate economic planning, though clearly enough no aspect of the tool-process is ever unplanned, but the possibility of planning sometimes being of an ill-considered nature cannot be ruled out. It is unconscious planning, determined more by custom and tradition than by active intelligence, that afflicts the tool process, yet there is at present a fear of attempts to deliberately employ intelligence, an emotional reaction by all accounts which is rationalized in two ways. Firstly, it is sometimes held that man's inability to take the important decisions concerning the organization and functioning of the economy is too well known, which sometimes leads to the conclusion, therefore, that man must not attempt at improving his ability deliberately but must leave such decisions to chance. That is man must live a life closely approximating ants and bees governed by conditioned reflexes: unseen, unreasoned, automatic. Such an approach of leaving such decisions to chance merely tends to entrench past problems even deeper and in no way solve them. Application of intelligence will induce man to learn to understand and to alleviate the problems.

> [Intelligence] is conversion of past experience into knowledge and projection of that knowledge in ideas and purposes that anticipate what may

> come to be in the future and that indicate how to realize what is desired. . . . The office of intelligence in every problem that either a person or a community meets is to effect a working connection between old habits, customs, institutions, beliefs, and new conditions.[7]

The second rationalization most commonly expressed in opposition to the deliberate use of intelligence in the area of economic planning is the old argument that it compromises freedom. So much has been written on the subject that suffice to say for the present that if the ultimate decisions rest in the authority of a democratic society, to change the representatives chosen on a temporary basis, to attempt economic policies designed to improve the functioning of the economy, it is a mistake to picture government as a heinous monster lurking in a shadowy lair and waiting to pounce upon and destroy the freedom of an innocent public.

The events unfolding in the East European countries in no way impairs the tenor of this argument, because the failure of the totalitarian regimes reflect, not the failure of planning *per se*, but the failure on the part of those in command to stress the appropriate areas, and appropriate extent, of planning mean total planning, which again is relapsing into a state of "intelligent blindness" which is precisely what this study attempts at de-emphasizing.

There is an increasing realisation that intelligence is superior to unreasoned habit (governed by conditioned reflexes) as a weapon with which to attack problems. The surplus problem in modern pecuniary societies is largely owing to the market system based upon a status hierarchy that fails to allow effective organization of the tool-process. The problem could be alleviated, as we have seen by a combination of monetary policy and fiscal policy designed to create new purchasing power to replace the purchasing power destroyed by the competition for tribute accumulation. Those in the high status groups could possibly be allowed to add to their collection of status symbols without permitting the continued concentration of status tribute to constrict the market and force the non-integration of men, technology, and materials. The market would be maintained at a high level by creating new status symbols at the same rate as the old status symbols were being eliminated from the market, which is tantamount to an extension of economic planning, and would, therefore invite opposition.

Thus, two alternatives appear to be available: either, blind habit can be relied upon and an economy of artificial scarcity and unnecessary hardship tolerated, *or*, intelligence can be made to bear upon the organization of the economy for the purpose of reducing the magnitude of the surplus problem. Either of the two alternatives will be beset with serious difficulties. If nothing is done about the surplus problem it will probably become more critical in the years ahead. And, of even greater significance is the possibility that the required economic restructuring will ultimately be caused in a disruptive manner, while leaving unimpaired all that is valuable in the existing order, would be virtually impossible.

Contrarily, if an attempt is made to tackle the problem that beset the world by deliberate application of intelligence (and not relying on unreasoned habit) care must be taken to avoid compromising individual and social freedom. A good deal of the opposition to attacking the surplus problem, with applied intelligence, emanates from the fear that the increased efficiency in the functioning of the tool-process will lead to such a general improvement in the conditions of low status groups that the relative rank of others may be seriously jeopardized. This need not necessarily be so, although to the extent that status is equalized, it becomes less inhibitive to the proper functioning of the tool-process. The welfare of the total society would improve and become secure. The freedom to accumulate tribute and status rank would not necessarily be reduced in any area, other than perhaps banking.

As conditions changed, the past society found it necessary, in order to alleviate certain problems, to use certain rules of behaviour. The fact that the traffic police stands at every major intersection does not reduce the freedom of anyone: it increases the freedom and security of all by ensuring orderly behaviour. It may be necessary, as certain problem areas become more critical and a solution is demanded by society, to install other "Stop" signs and to remove from some technical functions the inhibiting status structure that is superimposed upon the tool-process.

NOTES

1. See Galbraith, J.K. : *American Capitalism: The Concept of Countervailing Power* (Boston : Houghton Miffien Co.) 1952.
2. Wiener, N. : *The Human Use of Human Resources* (Boston: Houghton Miffien Co.) 1950, p. 171.
3. For long the poverty debate in India revolved around the determination of an appropriate calorie intake. See for

instance V.K.R.V. Rao:

The average calorie intake in developed countries is about 3300 calories per capita, whereas in the developing countries it in a little over 2000 calories per capita. See for an excellent discussion of these issues Chapter 5 entitled "Mass Poverty and Destitution", in Shaghil, M.: *The World Economic Order* (New Delhi: Cosmo Publications) 1989.

4. In our sense this may be deemed as under-consumption. See Sajal Mukherjee : *Theories of Under-consumption and Under-developed Countries,* Unpublished Ph.D. dissertation, 1989, Ranchi University, Ranchi.
5. For a discussion of some of the issues see Mukherjee Amitava : *The Economic Theory of Human Resources* (New Delhi: Indus Publishing Co.) 1990.
6. See for mechanics of this Subrata Ghatak: *Monetary Economics in Developing Countries* (London and Basingstoke: The Macmillan Press) 1981.
7. Dewey, J.: *Liberalism and Social Action* (New York: G.P. Putnam's Sons) 1955, p. 50

APPENDIX – A

SURPLUS PROBLEM IN AGRICULTURE AND ITS SOLUTION: An Interim Analysis

Political Ideology

It is imperative that intelligent attempts to solve the surplus problem be made immediately, and developed countries can ignore the problem only at the peril of submergence in a social revolution on a world scale. A majority of the world's population who live lives of poverty and privation have become dissatisfied and impatient with existing conditions of poverty and are demanding that whole-hearted programmes of improvement be initiated without further delay.[1] In recent past, world social forces have brought the collapse of several governments which could not recognize and effectively attack the surplus problem. Indeed similar forces led to the founding of the world government could nearly half a century ago, based upon the principle that all men should be allowed to participate in the functioning tool-process.[2] The weakening of this world government does not augur well for all democratic and peace loving people all over the world, because if it could be strengthened it could have become a valuable democratic instrumentality through which exceedingly effective attacks can be made on the problem of surpluses.

Several proposals have been put forward in the past as to the manner in which the problem of surplus should be attacked, and the myriad policy proposals that had emerged are divisible into at least two basic political theories: *one*, of the political ideologies that envision a type of society that has been identified by the term "democracy", and *two*, the subjugation of man to a totalitarian regime, which is as ancient as society itself and is based upon the assumption that the majority of people are incapable of sharing equally in the decisions of the life-process.

We shall take the second theory first in view of the exciting things that have happened and are happening in Eastern Europe and the USSR. It is maintained that the people need a strong leader to give them direction, security, and unity. Insofar as the importance of individual freedom is recognised it is relegated to the future as a luxury that cannot yet be afforded.

Because of the economic and political immaturity of the people at large, so the theory goes, the present need is to educate the people about obedience to the elite who have somehow obtained greater maturity, and unification of the people by the leader (even by means of force if necessary), and the transition to a more efficient productive process is completed and greater security from capricious nature and opposing ideas secured, so that the people can be taught the necessary facts of freedom and democracy.

The inherent fallacy in the *totalitarian* theory is that it has grounded itself on the false premise that the end justifies the use of any means whatever, which is erroneous because it embodies the unacceptable corollary that "any means can be employed to reach any desired end". The corollary is unacceptable because the concept of cultural continuity has brought the realisation that whatever means are employed directly determine the end actually realised. That totalitarian means are not the paths to a more effective democracy is evidenced by their belief in an initial period of supreme authority of a strong leader and the elimination of virtually all vestiges of a democratic and "free" society.

The democratic super-structure like all other cultural elements, was born out of the development from previous cultural elements, which cannot grow directly out of the unified and controlled State. The people can prepare for democracy only by beginning with the idea of freedom in all forms (political as well as economic)[3] and gradually learning the way to its realisation, and the amount of freedom will expand as the people become more aware of the nature of democracy and more adept at solving problem through a democratic framework. Democracy will not result from solving problems by the means of omnipotent authority and then suddenly be pouring upon the people freedom enjoining that they may no longer depend upon their leader to take decisions on their behalf and that they may no longer offer required implicit obedience.

The ultimate result of the totalitarian regime, as evidenced in the history of Ancient Egypt and Mesopotamia, among other societies, in the past led to feudalism: once the leader is no longer able to retain absolute power a number of leaders divided the empire. Out of feudalism democracy can grow, as it did in Greece and Europe, because where the "idea of freedom" substitutes the "idea of supreme authority", the way is open for the gradual emergence of democracy, but, contrarily, if the idea of authority retains its hold, the way is open for the strongest feudal leader to re-establish the totalitarian regime, as it occurred twice in Ancient Egypt and in modern USSR.

Neither the supporters of totalitarian regimes, at least those who seek an ultimate democracy, a large part of the economically destitute peoples of the world nor recognize the inherent fallacy in the totalitarian theory, of course. Many of the poverty stricken areas of the world tend to believe even now that the protagonists of the "left" are aware of poverty, of social and economic problems, of the oppression of a power-status system that denies to some the right to become integrated into the tool-process, and that the democrats or those who do not pin their faith in the "left", are not only unaware of such problems, but that they represent the oppressing high power-status groups. Communists maintain despite the great debacle in Eastern Europe, that the totalitarian system they advocated has its *raison d'etre* in such problems -- that their purpose is to produce a higher standard of living for the economically retarded peoples everywhere.

The claims of the communists were initially strengthened by the fact that they could raise the standard of living to a certain extent in a very short time by destroying the institutions that inhibit the use of modern technology. Of course, they fail to impress upon the economically destitute areas the severe limitations of their system, and now most communists would perhaps have begun to think that the long-run solution to social and economic problems must lie with democracy or at least in a system which is not totalitarian. They, however, refuse to concede that it is not possible to achieve an initial advantage by the totalitarian method before the people are given freedom, and if it is found true that the totalitarian method of attacking the surplus problem achieves more rapid initial results (a fact which is yet to be conclusively proved), recent history has also proved that it is also true that the horizons of the democratic method are unlimited. Taking a long term perspective view, it can be seen that whereas, if the problems are attacked by means of democratic processes, future progress, at an accelerating rate, is achievable, the totalitarian method will in all probability lead eventually to disorganisation and the necessity of making a new start as is being done the batious of communism of Eastern Europe and the Soviet Union. Thus, the surest way of improving the integration and coordination of the tool-process, in the long run if not in the short run, is the uninterrupted development of political as well as economic democracy.

Some still maintain the world social conflict is between the old order, which is characterised by poverty, and the new order, which is characterised by rapidly improving conditions. It is the responsibility of the democracies the world over to prove that this is a misconception. The controversy is between two alternative methods of attacking social and economic problems, and unless the developed countries embark upon a strong positive programme designed to alleviate all aspects of the existing surplus problem (in the developed as well as in all other parts of the world) a far greater portion of the world's population will ultimately be forced to believe that their salvation lies in seeking a solution to the problem under a totalitarian regime, and that the current failure of the system is an aberration which will correct itself in due course.

The developed and developing countries, together, has to establish that democratic solution to the problem of integrating and coordinating men, technology, and materials into a functioning tool-process is to seek progress. To invariably support the existing order in the areas of relative poverty that have not already accepted the philosophy of Marx and Lenin is to appear to deny the existence of the surplus problem. The success of the left tactics up to a point in the recent past had produced a fear bordering on hysteria among many people in the developed West, as a consequence of which, policies were framed that have served to diminish the confidence in democratic super-structure that formerly prevailed in other parts of the world.

The ideological controversy seemingly will be won in Asia not with cannon (as was attempted at Tianamen Square in China) but with a superior solution to the problem of poverty, which is not to say that force should not be used to oppose force, but that it should not be used to oppose economic and social change.[4] If the change takes undesirable paths, it must be opposed with superior alternatives. The developed countries, with its periodic financial panics, depressions, slums, and wasted effort, cannot influence less highly industrialised nations solely by offering themselves as an example to be followed. People who have known only poverty are not interested in the number of Tayotas and Robots enjoyed by the Japanese or number of fuel efficient vehicles that are in use by the American; they are interested in food and other necessities for themselves. It is not enough to point out that the capitalistic system has provided the world's highest standard of living (a claim denied by Sweden, among others). The economically destitute societies will observe the poverty and slums that still exist in many developed societies such as England and the U.S., and seek another system that will eliminate all such poverty in their own countries. The developed countries can effectively further the spread of democratic ideas and free enterprise ideal only by developing superior ideas, not by suppressing them.

The democracies in the developed parts of the world can further the development of world democracy by a frank admission of the existence of a surplus problem (both in the West and in the East) and by an attempt at showing to the underdeveloped countries how their own problems of surplus can be alleviated and how a better way of life through the use of democratic principles can be created. An analysis of the surplus problem and an evaluation the policies that have been suggested as solutions are the first steps in this regard, for only then it may be possible to determine the best course to be taken in the future by the poor and hungry peoples of the world. It should not be assumed, of course, that "intelligence will ever dominate the course of events; (not even) that it will save from ruin and destruction". But some procedure has to be tried. . . . To claim that intelligencc is a better method than its alternatives, authority, imitation, caprice and ignorance, prejudice and passion, is hardly an excessive claim".[5]

Surplus in Agriculture: Historical Perspective

That a surplus problem exists in the developed countries has been seen best perhaps by people whose primary interest has been in agriculture, and because more has been done to reveal the nature of the surplus problem in the developed countries, it can best be illustrated by a study of the tactics used in attempts to alleviate the problem of surplus in agriculture, which will provide some indication of the policies that may be adopted by under-developed and developing countries.

The earliest recognition of a surplus problem in agriculture in developed countries, notably the U.S., was caused by a decline of tobacco prices in England in early seventeenth century. It is true that agriculture in that part of the world remained primarily self-sufficient until the third and fourth decades of the 19th century but tobacco was produced by the Southern colonies for export to England as early as 1712, and it seems the tobacco farmers had anticipated by two centuries, the farmer movements that were to be witnessed in the 19th century. The general perception of the surplus problem in the 17th century was that the market system of distribution of agricultural goods was unable to absorb the increasing agricultural output (in this case tobacco) at prices acceptable to the Southern farmers. The colonial tobacco growers attempted at solving the problem through the establishment of legal minimum prices, artificially pinning down output, destroying tobacco inventory, and standardisation of the product to improve the quality and marketability of the product.

General concern for the surplus problem emerged during the transition of agriculture from self-sufficiency to commercialisation in the 4th and 5th decades of the 19th century. Till such time as agriculture was primarily self-sufficient, the former depended upon their own efforts and output for most of their consumption and not much of farm commodities were produced for consumption of others. As a national concomitant they conceived all of their problems as purely personal problems, and no basis existed for the development of concepts of an overall problem of agriculture, but with the transition of agriculture from self-sufficiency to commercialisation, agriculturists started depending on much of their consumption basket and their reliance on a market to sell that portion of their produce which they did not consume on the farm began. This change in the pattern of agriculture forced upon the farmers the thought that agriculturists as a group had common problems that demanded the attention of agriculture as a whole.

The cause of the problem in the 1830s and 1840s was thought of as the monopoly power of the middlemen, and low agricultural prices were attributed to the speculators, who arbitrarily fixed low prices to be paid to the farmers but once the farmers had marketed their produce, prices were raised to reap profits. Warehouse operators, commission agents, and other middlemen were accused of exaction of monopoly fees from the farmers, and for confiscating a part of the ultimate price of farmers' produce paid by the consumers. The railroads were particularly attacked for establishing uniform monopoly prices by combining into trusts (a variant of modern cartels), for issuing worthless watered stock, and for bribing and influencing legislators and other public servants.

The solutions proposed for the problem so conceived usually took the garb of what modern day socialists would urge, namely, government control or ownership of transportation, storage, and processing facilities; direct trade between the farmer and the consumer by elimination of the middleman; a return to the state of self-sufficiency to the extent possible; and cooperative processing and marketing by farmers. It was believed that avoidance of monopoly exploitation by the middlemen would guarantee an adequate price for any amount of agricultural produce.

Subsequent solutions for solving the problem of monopoly exploitation dropped the proposal for a return to self-sufficiency, and instead the need for concerted action by the farmers as a group received greater emphasis. Some legislation to regulate the railroads and other groups which were seen by the agriculturists as unsocial monopolies, was passed in earlier decades, but it was primarily during 1870s and 1880s that state controls were imposed to eliminate such practices as pooling, monopoly pricing, discrimination, and exorbitant interest charges. This period also saw the acceptance of the cooperative movement and cheap money proposals as means to attack the farm problem.

The proposal for a return to direct trade between the agriculturists and the eventual consumer was based on the hope that the costly services of specialists in transportation, storage, and marketing could be eliminated. Direct trade was to be realised by the establishment of cooperative and arrangement for co-operative marketing had been made in the dairy industry as early as 1810, and by the time of the American Civil War, the cooperative movement had expanded to a position of some importance, but the war resulted in the almost complete disappearance of farmers' cooperatives. Then, in the period of unrest following the war, the cooperative movement reappeared with more vigour than ever, but at least partly as a result of the inability of the farmers to eliminate the technical functions that developed with the specialised economy and became interposed between the farm and consumer or industrial manufacturers, the cooperative movement underwent another period of decline in the 1890s.

Combined with the cooperative movement in the

period of general agitation against the privileged position of the middlemen, were proposals for relieving the farm problem through the issuance of more money: the period of the 1870s and 1880s can best be characterised as a period of conflict between debtor and creditor. The farmers, as a group, were debtors and they attributed their hardships to the scarcity of money.

When the farmer needed money with which to meet his interest and tax costs or to purchase non-farm commodities it seemed to be very scarce. When it became necessary to repay a loan, the amount of money to be paid had become the equivalent of twice the amount of farm produce it could have purchased at the time the loan was availed of. These conditions seemed to the farmers, who had accepted the quantity theory of money, to be the result of insufficient currency.

Of equal importance with the amount of money in circulation, in the views of the farmers, was the ability of the banks and credit lenders to vary the amount at will. The farmers noted that the prices of farm commodities fluctuated during the year, such that at the time the crops were marketed by the farmers, prices were low, but after the farmers had relinquished their ownership of the crop, prices rose again. Such price fluctuations were attributed to an inefficient monetary system that did not expand at the time money was needed most; to the action of non-farm groups who controlled prices and credit; and to the need of the farmers, who almost invariably had mortgaged their crop in order to meet their obligations and obtain seed, to market the crop as soon as possible after harvesting.

The farmers were convinced that one of the most important causes of the depressed condition of agriculture was the scarcity and inelasticity of currency, and that the solution to their problem was government creation of new money. During the period from 1868 to 1896 various proposals were offered for farmers as the way to, obtain higher prices for farm products and relief from their debts through cheap money and inflation. The more conservative proposals included unlimited free coinage of silver, devaluation of the content of existing money, and government creation of notes to be loaned on land pledged as security. The more radical proposals included unlimited creation of irredeemable paper money and government issuance of silver certificates in an amount equal to the estimated value of gold and silver existing in the mountains of the United States. Three of the plans enjoyed an appreciable following.

During the first two decades of this century the farmers again turned to the theory that the farm problem resulted from the monopoly exploitation by processors and merchandisers, but unlike in earlier periods, an awareness of the significance of the change from self-sufficient to commercialised agriculture was discernible. Instead of harping, therefore, on the presence, of a number of middlemen, agitation was now directed at marketing inefficiency and exploitation by local buyers, and the solution proposed was again the establishment of farmers' cooperatives, which saw a period of rapid growth in the number of local cooperative organisations.

The new cooperative movement got underway primarily on the belief that if the arbitrary price-setting of local buyers could be circumvented, the competitive national price would be high enough to ensure a fair return to the farmers, and the cooperative organisations of this period attempted to market all of the goods produced by the farmers in a local area. Because the cooperatives were organised around the supply of goods produced by the farmers locally, rather than the market, the cooperative made no appreciable dent on prices, which warranted the revision in the programme and a new stage was set in the treatment of the problem.

It was only after World War I that cooperative marketing generally changed to commodity lines from local goods, because of the importance of commodity cooperatives in controlling the amount of a good that was placed in the market in any given period and thereby avoid a glut the market. Emphasis was on an orderly market, and not on eliminating the middleman. The belief, however, remained that the national price would be high enough to ensure a fair return for all output levels if efficient marketing at the national level could be attained, and the control of output of any given good by an overall marketing agency was conceived of as the only way to achieve efficient marketing over a national area, because, so it was thought, as long as agricultural output was marketed by individual farmers or by local cooperatives, the crop would be marketed so hurriedly that it would cause a glut in the market with supply exceeding demand and prices would plunge down. It was believed that this was avoidable if the organisation of the farmers into national cooperatives along commodity lines could be established, for that would permit orderly marketing all round the year and prices could be maintained at a high level.

As discussed above, the farm leaders regretted that farmers had to sell of their crops as quickly as possible to obtain the funds needed to meet their obligations, and, therefore, some means had to be found for providing the individual farmers with the required funds to enable them to hold on to their stocks of farm produce and thereby delay the marketing of their crop till they could get remunerative prices. This had given way to some agitation for government aid, but most of the farmers were not well disposed towards direct government intervention, the agrarian self-help philosophy remained predominant, and the farmers sought to solve their problem of prices and fair return through cooperatives. The generally accepted mechanism was that the cooperatives advanced a substantial part of the value of a crop to the farmer at the time of harvesting, stored the crop in warehouses and unloaded it on to the market gradually over the period of a year, and when the crop had been fully marketed, the final payment was made to the farmer. This was seemingly quite successful for a time, but the record wheat crop of 1925 and the output of cotton in 1926 in the U.S., was too large for even orderly marketing to distribute at favourable prices and the cooperatives found after the price fall of 1926 that they had advanced the farmers more on their crops than were realizeable from the sale of the farm produce. The bankrupt cooperatives failed in their attempts to regulate the flow of farm commodities until the U.S. Government came to their rescue. The Federal Government of the U.S., accepted the debts of the cooperatives and for a time attempted to finance them in further experiments with orderly marketing, but it was soon found that more and more farm products to be bought and stored in order to maintain the cooperatives: in three years, one billion bushels of wheat and one and one-third million bales of cotton were accumulated in the store-houses, and even then prices continually declined.

Government Intervention for Restricting Output

The failure of the orderly marketing theory brought on the new interpretation of the problem that the problem would have to be solved by government intervention, which belief has remained intact in years of low prices even to the present day almost world wide. Years of prosperity, however, witnessed the return to the philosophy of self-help and government programmes are relegated to the background as infringements of individual freedom and sound business principles.

The solutions to the problem of agricultural surpluses that gained pre-eminence during the 1930s attributed the relatively depressed conditions of agriculture to over-production. During the depression, therefore, the major emphasis was given to programmes seeking a reduction in the output of the basic agricultural commodities, because, so ran the arguments, farm prices dropped first and farthest in times of recession, because non-agricultural producers hacked back output to maintain relatively high prices, while farmers, acting individually, failed to contain aggregate farm production to levels that would help in maintaining relatively high prices. The only way, therefore, to maintain a relatively high price for agricultural produce was restriction of agricultural production imposed by the Government to correspond to variations in the market and non-agricultural production. Because individual farmers could not use the methods of non-agricultural producers to vary their output, the function of achieving control over agricultural production was given over to the government, by welding the more than six million farm businesses then obtaining in the U.S. into a monopoly group. The government, with the voluntary cooperation of the producers of a few basic farm commodities, established acreage quotas and paid direct subsidies to those farmers that cooperated by planting only their quota of acres in the controlled commodities.

The cotton and tobacco farmers and subsequently other farmers as well sought for compulsory marketing quotas. Because nothing prevented the farmer from producing as much on the restricted number of acres as they produced before on a larger number of acres, by use of fertilisers and other methods; and because the farmers who did not adhere to production controls could increase their output and offset the efforts of acreage restriction by cooperating farmers, it soon became apparent that penalty for marketing of crops in excess of the quotas was necessary, apart from restricting the acres on which it was grown. Subsidy payments to farmers for soil conservation practices was introduced, provided they participated in the marketing control programmes.

Government Intervention for Support Price

Attempts to increase agricultural prices in the 1930s also made use of support prices and orderly marketing. The government established a floor prices for some commodities by agreeing to purchase or to make loans on all the output that could not be sold at or above a prescribed price level. While the loans served the purpose of enabling the farmers to delay the marketing of their crops to avoid flooding the market with farm produce at harvest time, direct purchases were directed towards levelling out the quantity of farm commodities available in years of good and years of bad harvest. The purchase programme was designed to raise prices but was sought to be justified, in part, by reference to the ancient oriental concept of the ever-normal granary. Loans plus direct purchases effectively set minimum prices for the commodities included in the programme.

The output in excess of that absorbed by the domestic market was to be diverted to alternative uses, one of which was relief doles, distributed through the Red Cross, school lunch programmes, stamp plans, and bread lines. These consumer subsidies were always the ostensible considerations, while the real consideration was to attempt at disposing off agricultural surpluses.

A very effective means employed to reduce the concentration of surplus goods was to dump them in foreign markets, which could not be employed too freely, however, for fear of retaliation by foreign countries.

An additional method employed to benefit the farmers was the use of direct parity payments. The goal sought by the farm programmes prior to 1936 was "parity prices", which were designed to re-establish parity between agricultural and industrial prices obtaining now with those that existed in some previous period, usually the period just before the World War I. The relationship that had existed between farm prices and the prices of certain other commodities purchased by the farmer, was established for a base year (which was a "normal" year) and the prices that would then provide "equality for agriculture" at subsequent years, would be the prices of agricultural goods which bore the same relationship with the current prices of commodities purchased by farmers. Parity payments, therefore, were direct subsidies to the farmers of a certain amount, per unit of output, designed to adjust current farm receipts to the level of parity prices.

After the great depression, the goal of "equality for agriculture" policies was more or less substituted by the goal of "parity of incomes". For parity prices the amount of certain crops marketed had to be cut down to such a low level that farm income would stagnate at a level. Parity income envisaged that per capita net farm income now will have the same relation to current per capita non-farm income, as was obtaining in some previous period of reference. Parity income was, however, difficult to operationalise in terms of policy formulation, and parity prices, therefore, continued as the effective goal for most price support schemes in agriculture.

Agricultural economists have disapproved the policy of attacking the surplus problem in agriculture by maintaining *status quo* in the pattern of agriculture and by containing agricultural output for achieving parity prices, because, the path to equality for agriculture, was not to maintain parity prices which overstated the relative value of farm commodities, but to cut down costs. Improvement in the relative income position of agriculture, so they believe, should be by reducing the number of farmers who must share the income accruing to agriculture. This line of thinking, which differed from the policy of parity prices or parity incomes pursued in the pre-depression days, is tantamount to a difference between policies designed to *save agriculture* and policies designed to save all the *individual farmers* now engaged in agricultural production. The foundation of farm policies under this dispensation is conceived of as the employment of a minimum number of farmers, using the most efficient accepted techniques, to produce that amount of food, feed, and fibre that, when sold in the market, will provide the same return on the investment of land, labour, capital and enterprise in agriculture, which is received by investments of similar land, labour, capital and enterprise in non-agricultural industries. That is, the return to investment of land, labour, capital and enterprise in agriculture must be at least equal to the return which can be secured on these factor inputs in alternative employment, which is the transfer price. Hark these words for one of the earliest statements of this line of reasoning:

> ". . . the surest path to the farmer's prosperity is through curtailment of production by reducing the number of farmers thereby giving each the benefits of volume of production at high prices, rather than through individual farm curtailment which would result in higher prices for a lower volume of production with operating charges remaining practically fixed, however."[6]

It is maintained that in attacking the problems of the agricultural sector from the perspective of saving the individual farmer the policies which subsidised the inefficient farm and placed undue restriction upon the efficient ones. Attempts at establishing either parity prices or parity income by production and marketing controls and by direct subsidies, the maladjustments of the past have been prolonged instead of inducing the required adjustments for correcting the basic causes that generated the problem of surpluses in agriculture. The concept of parity prices was based inherently on the unrealistic assumption that the proper relations now between various agricultural prices and between agricultural and non-agricultural prices are the relationships that existed in some past period between them. Given that the price or income relations of the past period were themselves the product of maladjustment, parity prices serve only to perpetuate inefficiencies. Raising agricultural prices through deliberate restriction of output is tantamount to transference of purchasing power from the hands of consumers to hands of the farmers without increasing the total amount of purchasing power available in the economy or without increasing the welfare of the society as a whole.

The positive proposals of this group of economists are derived from breaking down the farm problem into the following three components:

(i) the problem of secular maladjustment of the agricultural sector to the total economy, emanating from the failure of the agricultural sector to decline as rapidly as is warranted by the relation of the supply of agricultural output to their demand;
(ii) the problem of the instability of farm income, resulting from the fluctuating market; and
(iii) the problem of poverty conditions, in which a segment of the farm population exists, emerging out of maladjustment of the agricultural sector to the total economy and from the status system of distribution.

It is held that the secular over-expansion of the agricultural sector was responsible for keeping the relatively worse off than non-agricultural prices and incomes. Because the demand for agricultural goods is relatively inelastic and because of the long-run increase in the efficiency of agriculture, the agricultural sector must successively shrink as a proportion of the total economy. Sufficient adjustments have not been made in the agricultural sector to the forces which caused to increase the supply of farm products more rapidly than the demand for agricultural produce, since the latter part of the nineteenth century.

Agricultural output per man, per acre, and agricultural output *per se*, in the aggregate has increased as a result of:

(i) technological improvements, such as soil science, the development of better breeds of plants and animals, substitution of machinery for feed consuming animals, improved skills, innovations that save labour or what A.K. Sen called "Landesque",[7] and the accumulation of more tools on the farms;
(ii) increase in the land under cultivation or in pasturage; and
(iii) increase in the farm population resulting from the unusually high reproduction rate of rural areas.

The demand for agricultural commodities, on the other hand, has increased at a slower rate due to:

(i) declining exports;
(ii) the inelasticity of food requirement with respect to improvements in the standard of living; and
(iii) competition from substitutable synthetic commodities.

A differential rate of change in the supply and demand of agricultural output has led to the development of the theory that in early days, the techniques of agriculture allowed such a limited return to each farmer that the great majority of the population was required to till the soil, enabling the pursuits of non-agricultural activities only when the productivity of agriculture increased sufficiently to release some of the workers from tilling the soil. Agriculture, thus, came to be regarded as the basic industry upon which society depended, and expansion of non-agricultural activities was merely a function of the efficiency of the agricultural activities, and, therefore, as efficiency in agriculture increases, the farmers who are replaced must out-migrate from agriculture into the non-agricultural sector, which explains why advancing technology enables the satisfaction of the needs for farm commodities with increasingly lesser number of farmers in the agricultural sector. However, granted this to be the basic nature of agriculture, no limit can be placed on the need for non-agricultural commodities of various types, and, therefore, the surplus farmers are to be absorbed into non-agricultural sector on a continuous basis, for the agricultural sector of the economy to be kept in proper balance with the total economy. The problem of surpluses in agriculture is, then, caused in part, by the failure of non-agricultural sector to expand as rapidly as is warranted by increased agricultural efficiency. Thus, this theory enjoins the surplus farmers are not absorbed into expanding non-agricultural industries at the rate which is commensurate with the rate of their displacement from agricultural sector on account of advances in agricultural technology. The supply of agricultural commodities, therefore, tend to expand more rapidly than does the demand for such goods, causing a relatively depressed prices and incomes situation. Thus, the genesis of the farm problem is improper balance between the agricultural and non-agricultural sectors of the economy, which is the same thing as asserting that proper balance has not been maintained between the supply of, and demand for, farm commodities, and a surplus farm population has arisen.

Surplus farm-labourers are not unemployed in the sense that characterizes industrial workers; they are under-employed and joins the rank of disguised unemployment.[8] Such under employment partakes the nature of inefficient utilisation of the time and efforts of the surplus farmers, which causes their incomes to be lower than the incomes of similar non-agricultural labourers. The proponents of the theory of insufficient agricultural adjustment maintain that underemployed agricultural labour evidences an inefficient allocation of resources because the marginal productivity of farm labour is below the marginal productivity of non-agricultural workers. Agricultural incomes are too low, therefore, because there are too many farmers working in the farms.

The solution to this problem of surpluses in agriculture lies in reducing the number of farmers and in concurrently increasing the amount of farm machinery in use, till the point is reached where the marginal productivity and income of land, labour and capital is equilibrated in the agricultural and non-agricultural sectors of the economy.

Those who subscribe to agricultural fundamentalism that the "noble profession" of agriculture dissuades those farmers living in conditions of poverty not to leave the land, is no longer valid. There are ample evidence of farm to non-farm sector migration under various circumstances. Even when the relative position of agricultural prices and incomes improved, there occurs a net migration out of the agricultural sector, and when the conditions of agriculture worsens (relatively speaking) there tends to be a net in-migration.[9] When non-agricultural employment opportunities are available, the surplus farmers automatically leave the farm, to return only when they are unable to obtain employment in the non-agricultural sector or what may be called the urban centres. The clearest expression of the philosophy underlying this phenomenon is best described in terms of the following instructions to a representative of the Department of Agriculture in the U.S.A., who had gone from Washington into the field on a survey: "You tell them jackasses down there that farming is a business. It ain't a way of life."

The solutions to solve the multi-dimensional farm problems, when interpreted as the insufficient adjustment of agriculture to the total economy, are not in conflict with each other. Efforts directed towards decreasing the number of farmers must not be neutralised by government subsidies and support prices which, in one sense, subsidize inefficient farmers, urging them to remain in agriculture. Efforts at reclaiming surplus land when agriculture is already over-expanded, and imparting advanced farming techniques to surplus farmers confounds the problem.

On the other hand, the theory requires that programme for the agricultural sector should encourage out-migration from agriculture. Surplus agricultural labourers should be taught other skills and knowledge to seek alternative employment in the non-farm sector and provided with assistance in obtaining such employment, urban housing, and the funds needed to implement the move. The advantages of urban opportunities should be put forth before the rural children and the rural birth rate should be decreased.

Apart from surpluses generated by the secular over-expansion of agriculture, market fluctuations which characterize capitalistic economies make things even worse. By and large, agricultural production is relatively stable, except that the vagaries of weather conditions may cause some gyrations but it is free from any form of production control, but demand for the agricultural commodities portray wide fluctuations. Thus, the supply of agricultural commodities is in a much greater surplus at some times than at others, resulting in fluctuations in farm income that cause hardship and make the utilisation of the principles of good business in agriculture a difficult proposition. The system of markets and prices is supposed to provide the basis for decision-making with regard to the allocation of resources, but the system of markets and prices, cannot serve this function where fluctuation in prices is so frequent and violent. It is, thus, not possible to anticipate the contours of given price or price relationship in future.

Proponents of theories here under discussion maintain that while the attempts of the 1930s to stabilize agricultural prices and incomes by varying agricultural output with the market did little to solve the farm problem, they inhibited solutions. Because agriculture is "mandated" to produce food and fibre as efficiently as possible, a stable farm output is desirable and programmes seeking stabilisation of prices by production and marketing controls, are in conflict with programmes directed at solving the problems of secular agricultural maladjustment.

Farmers in Underdeveloped Countries

Experts who view farm problem as a problem of too many farmers chasing "too little land", in contradiction to earlier attempts directed towards improving the relative position of agricultural incomes, favour the maintenance of a stable agricultural output leaving prices to be determined by the system of markets and prices, and the stabilisation of farm incomes by means of compensatory government subsidies, to be used to make good the difference between actual market prices and support prices that have been determined in advance of the growing period.

The support prices declared in advance partakes the nature of "forward prices", and provide farmers with an opportunity which is akin to that available to the agricultural producers for making allocation decisions in terms of the anticipated relations between costs and prices. Support prices of this genre will, therefore, encourage needed adjustments in agriculture, and not perpetuate past maladjustments, and the principles of good business practice can be brought to bear upon the agricultural sector as well. Such support prices help stabilize agricultural incomes without pricing farm goods out of the market. Agricultural output will be consumed, and not added to the accumulation of surplus goods, because all of agricultural output will be sold in the market at whatever prices can be obtained, that is, agriculture would become a perfectly competitive industry or nearly so.

In setting the support prices, care has to be taken to set it at such a level that overvaluing agricultural commodities is avoided. If the support prices for agricultural goods are set too high they will encourage the continued over-expansion of agriculture and conflict with solutions to the problem of secular maladjustment. Attempts to use programmes similar to these proposals, in the latter 1940s and 1950s have been criticised, all over the world, as setting support prices too high in keeping with obsolete ideas of parity. If the agricultural support prices are pegged at too high a level, they will place an undue burden upon the total economy, which is why for agricultural goods support prices must be set at the approximate level, where agricultural prices would have been determined by forces of demand and supply, if the market had not declined. The support prices are only required to stabilize farm incomes (not maintain them at an unrealistic artificial level) at the central value about which it tends to fluctuate. Parity concepts look to the past and inhibit the continual out-migration of agricultural labour to bring forth the correlations in the maladjustments in the agricultural sector, with the total economy.

Subsidies should be provided for stabilising agricultural out-migration, rather than to encourage surplus farmers to remain on the land. Agricultural price supports should not be provided for just any level of output in the agricultural sector but to the extent necessary to supply the "normal" demands of the market. The amount of each crop to be subsidised is the amount that would be produced if agriculture were in proper adjustment to the total economy, which would cause the competition of the efficient farmers to drive the inefficient farmers out of agriculture and bring about the needed adjustment.

The most careful proposal for a subsidy programme designed to stabilize farm incomes in the face of a fluctuating market without inhibiting the adjustment of the agricultural sector to the total economy would include a crop quota, that is to be subsidised, without there being individual quotas to subsidize inefficiency while requiring a substantial restriction by efficient farmers. Where the actual output in the economy should be greater than the quota, the entire crop would be sold at the market price, and if the price received was less than the support-price, every producer who sells in the market would receive subsidies, on the amount he marketed equal to the ratio of crop quota and actual output in the economy times what he has actually sold, to make good the difference between the market price and the support price. Farmers would receive subsidy for only the surplus two-thirds of the crop, and subsidy would then be lowered each year until the equilibrium price was reached, where the amounts produced and sold were absorbed in the market at prices that would provide equal incomes to both agricultural and non-agricultural labour of equal skill and ability, having access to the same amount of factor inputs.

The subsidy payments would not be made in cash: they would be credited to each farmer and could be claimed only when spent for approved practices. Thus, subsidy payments would not serve to subsidize inefficiency and would not encourage surplus farmers to remain in agriculture. Subsidy payments could be used only to increase the efficiency of the farm unit or to enable the inefficient farmer to leave agriculture and acquire or learn some other skill for alternative employment in the non-farm sector. Acceptable improvements, apart from those resulting in out-migration from agriculture, would be, *inter alia*, better equipment, expansion in the size of inefficient small farms, and aid in planning the operation of the farm.

In case the scheme advocated by the proponents of the approach to the farm problem seeking appropriate adjustment of agriculture to the total economy were successful, a cut in agricultural output caused by the out-migration of farmers would ensure up to the point where "normal" market prices would equilibrate returns for the same marginal productivity in agricultural sector and non-agricultural sector. And then, stability in farm incomes would be brought about by compensatory subsidies, despite farm prices being allowed to fluctuate with the market, to eliminate the possibility of accumulation of surplus goods, but a portion of the population in the agricultural sector might still exist in conditions of relative poverty. Furthermore, during the interregnum when adjustments are being worked out, the surplus farmers yet to migrate out of the agriculture sector, would suffer from paucity of housing, medical care, education, food, and other needs. To facilitate the adjustment to fully work itself out in agriculture, production subsidies of the varieties used in the past need to be discontinued: the surplus farmer need not be subsidised to remain in agricultural sector, but society cannot leave him uncared to starve, which problem, the advocates of the theory of integrated agriculture, would deem as lying in the domain of a problem of welfare.

As Schultz has emphasised,[10] the system of markets and prices can be used either for the efficient allocation of resources, or it can be used to increase the welfare of the society by a more egalitarian distribution of income in society. Any attempt at employing the system of markets and prices to accomplish both tasks concurrently is doomed to failure with regard to accomplishing either. Therefore, the use of the system of markets and prices is urged to induce the efficient allocation of resources, and some other means may be devised to solve the problem of increasing societal welfare through an efficient distribution of income in the economy.

A very important solution suggested to tackle the

problem of distribution by the economists advocating this solution of the farm problem, relates to the use of consumer subsidies. Mid-day meals in schools, in-plant feeding programmes, food distribution plans, and other forms of "transfer payments-in-kind" are generally cited at the possible channels for providing consumer subsidies. Along with these, social security benefits like Contributory Provident Fund, survivors benefits, and educational and medical benefits are further suggestions as to the channels of attack on the residual societal problems of poverty and surplus, that would persist were the agricultural sector of the economy to be reduced to the level determined by the market distributive system.[11]

NOTES

1. This was one reason which impelled the Secretary General of the United Nations to observe in 1983: "The State of the World Economy . . . has never looked more . . . despairing", as quoted in M. Shaghil : *The World Economic Order* (New Delhi : Cosmo Publications) 1989, p. 107.
2. The United Nations Charter reads, *inter alia,*

   We the Peoples
   of the United Nations
   ....
   ....
   to promote social progress
   and *better standards of life*
   in larger freedom
   ....
   Have resolved to combine our
   efforts to accomplish these aims.

   Accordingly, our respective Government
   ....
   have agreed to the present Charter
   of the United Nations and do hereby

establish an inter-national organisation
to be known as the United Nations.
(*Emphasis ours*)

3. This has been the Indian stand throughout of post-independence struggle for economic development.
4. See the seminal work of R.P. Misra : *Development Issues of Our Time* (New Delhi : Concept Publishing Co.) 1985.
5. J. Dewey : *Experience and Nature* (Boston : Putnam's Sons) 1935, p. 437.
6. C.A. Wiley : "Agriculture and the Disparity in Prices", *The Southern Political and Social Science Quarterly* Vol. VI, March 1926, p. 13.
7. See Sukhomoy Chakravaty : *Development Planning* (New Delhi : Oxford University Press) 1985, and Anne Booth and R.M. Sundrum : *Labour Absorption in Agriculture* (Delhi : Oxford University Press)1984.
8. The Discussion on disguised unemployment relevant to our them is in Shigeru Ishikawa : *Labour Absorption in Asian Agriculture* (Geneva : I.L.O., ARTEP) 1981 reprint, distributed by Maruzen Asia Pvt. Ltd., Singapore, pp. 69-74.
9. The issues of in migration has attracted considerable attention of economists, but these are in the nature of problems and policies related to rural urban migration.
10. Theodre W. Schultz: *Investing in People : The Economics of Population Quality* (Berkeley and Los Angeles : University of California Press) 1981.
11. The issue of farm subsidies now have assumed international proportions. The United States wants the E.E.C. Countries to cut expert subsidy by 90 per cent and internal subsidy by 79 per cent, whereas E.E.C. countries have agreed to reduce subsidy and support prices by 30 percent. The disagreement of this issue may even cause a breakdown of the of the Uruguay Round of G.A.T.T. negotiations. See *Economic Times*, New Delhi, 2nd December 1990 and *Times of India*, 1st December 1990.

INDEX